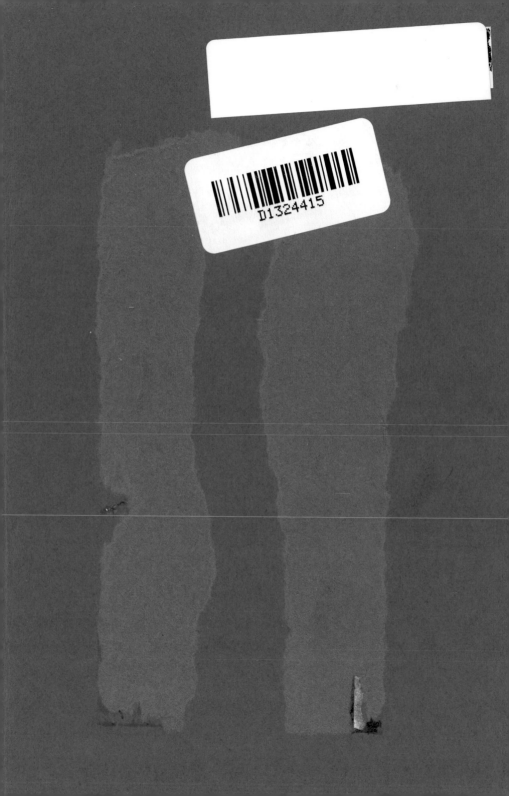

SEX
WITHOUT
SHAME

Encouraging
the Child's
Healthy Sexual
Development

SEX WITHOUT SHAME

Encouraging the Child's Healthy Sexual Development

By ALAYNE YATES, M.D.

WILLIAM MORROW AND COMPANY, INC.

NEW YORK   1978

Library of Congress Cataloging in Publication Data

Yates, Alayne.
    Sex without shame.

    Bibliography: p.
    1. Children—Sexual behavior. I. Title.
HQ784.S45Y37   649'.1   78-997
ISBN 0-688-03301-6

BOOK DESIGN   CARL WEISS

Printed in the United States of America.

First Edition

1 2 3 4 5 6 7 8 9 10

TO MY SEXY CHILDREN:

MIMI, MARA, EVE, WENDY, MOSES, SARA, STEVE

KRISTI, RICK, JILL, DONNA, DAVE, AND PAM

WHO TAUGHT ME MOST OF WHAT I KNOW

CONTENTS

PART I

**UNDERSTANDING THE CHILD'S
SEXUALITY**

PART II

ENRICHING THE CHILD'S SEXUAL
RESPONSE

PART I

UNDERSTANDING THE CHILD'S SEXUALITY

I

SENSUOUS CHILDREN?

A cantaloupe sky signals the nearness of dawn as the two bare bodies again stretch upon the satin comforter. He nuzzles her skin, breathes her racy scent, and quickly rouses. He inhales deeply, presses urgently against her, and unwittingly pinches her nipple in the process. Flinching slightly, she rubs his nose and whispers softly. He fixes his eyes on her, and kneads one delectable tidbit with his fingers as he relishes the other with his lips. She pushes firmly on his nates as he forces his hips aganist hers. An ancient rhythm oscillates and ebbs. Gradually his grip relaxes and he drifts toward a deep, refreshing slumber. She tenderly disentangles her hair from beneath his body. Then she covers him with the comforter, and carries him to his crib.

The infant is a sensuous being who is capable of experiencing a crescendo of pleasure with each feeding. Triggered by odor, exquisitely responsive to touch, greedy and aggressive, the infant searches desperately, claims his prize, and melts into languid slumber. Boundaries dissolve in oceanic oneness. Why is cupid always portrayed as an infant? To be in love is to reexperience infancy. The infant owns his mother totally, and cares not for any other. If she denies him, he is instantly enraged. He is encapsulated by his neediness—

for touch, for scent, for food, for warmth. His whole body is a sexual organ. Many years ago Freud remarked, "Can anyone who has seen an infant sinking back satiated from the breast with a smile escape the thought that this represents the forerunner of later, specifically sexual, satisfaction?"

The famous sex researcher William Masters was first an obstetrician. He relieved the monotony of delivery after delivery by devising a game that he played with the newborn boys. He described the contest succinctly: "Can I get the cord cut before the kid has an erection?" He won only half the time. Innumerable baby boys were born with fully erect organs. He also noted that all girl babies lubricated vaginally in the first four to six hours of life. Infants were born ready and fully equipped. During sleep, spontaneous erections or vaginal lubrications occur every eighty to ninety minutes throughout the entire life span. (Masters, 1975)* Throughout life, sleeping sexual function remains far more reliable. While awake, our conscious anxieties take their toll.

Masturbation culminating in climax may occur as early as the first month of life. The baby girl is the most enthusiastic and proficient. With unmistakable intent, she crosses her thighs rigidly. With a glassy stare she grunts, rubs, and flushes for a few seconds or minutes. If interrupted, she screams with annoyance. Movements cease abruptly and are followed by relaxation and deep sleep. This sequence occurs many times during the day, but only occasionally at night. The baby boy proceeds with distinct penis throbs and thrusts accompanied by convulsive contractions of the torso. After climax his erection (without ejaculation) quickly subsides and he appears calm and peaceful. Kinsey reports that one boy of eleven months had ten climaxes in an hour and that another of the same age had fourteen in thirty-eight minutes.

Infants intrigued by erotic sensations are neither emotionally ill nor stunted in development. Harry Bakwin, pe-

---

* Full references appear in the Bibliography, which begins on p. 231.

diatrician, presents the following case of a daughter of a physician:

At about seven months of age she took a great fancy to dolls. She would press her body against a large rag doll to which she was very attached and make rhythmic movements. The movements at first took place only in the evening at bedtime. At one year of age she and the doll became inseparable. She carried this doll about with her all day and from time to time would throw the doll on the floor, lie down on top of it, and rhythmically press her body against it, "as in the sexual act," according to her parents. Attempts to distract her during these episodes caused screaming. She would cling to the doll until she felt satisfied. The parents thought that she "completed an orgasm in her own way." By about fifteen months of age the episodes had decreased in frequency and were of shorter duration and by seventeen months the masturbation took place only at bedtime. When heard from at four and one half years, she was to all appearances a normal child. Her mother described her as alert, bright, and vivacious . . . at present she is a medical student.

Thirty-six percent of year-old infants are reported by their mothers to play with their genitals. (Newson, 1968) Between two and three years, many more youngsters masturbate, and pleasuring is already commoner in boys than girls. Nursery school children show an avid interest in each other's genitals and initiate erotic experiments. Half of all middle-class preschoolers indulge in sex play or masturbation. (Sears, 1957) Games such as "Mommy and Daddy" or "Doctor" are common by age four. (Newson, 1968) By age five most children have asked questions about sex, and know that boys have a penis but girls do not. (Kreitler, 1966). From the age of three, little girls recognize themselves as certainly female, and little boys recognize themselves as certainly male. (Rutter, 1971) (Money, 1961)

Between three and six, children raised in traditional homes gather about themselves the accouterments of the male or female role. Little girls play house, enjoy dolls, and draw figures with rounded contours. Boys choose active toys and construct drawings with points, angles, and moving objects. Girls are now much less sexually active than boys.

A curious modification arises at about the time when children enter school. Sexual activity declines, so that at age seven only ten percent of boys masturbate, indicating that most of those who did masturbate have relinquished sexual pleasure. Only five percent are engaged in sex play with girls. (Ramsey, 1943) This sudden repression of sexuality is the beginning of a period called "latency." There are no hormonal or growth changes which account for this rapid shift. In cultures such as the Arandas of Central Australia, children continue to masturbate and show avid interest in sex throughout maturation. (Roheim, 1974) In some segments of our own culture, such as certain communes and slums, eroticism continues to increase. The answer, of course, rests in our method of child rearing.

Another sign of underlying discomfort is the predominance of aggressive fantasies about sex. A glimpse of coitus or sounds from the parents' room at night are construed as "Daddy is beating Mommy." A five-year-old who sees his parents kissing passionately says loudly, "Don't do that, it isn't nice!" One half of the five-year-olds assume that mother's abdomen must be cut open in order to remove the baby. (Kreitler, 1966) About a third of children five and over believe that girls first have a penis but then lose it somehow; it shrinks or is cut off. One third, more boys than girls, have castration fantasies. (Conn, 1947) In the five-and-up age group it is extremely unusual for a boy to say something nice about his penis. When asked, "What is your penis like, good, bad or . . . ?" little boys try to cover themselves, act perplexed, or make a statement such as "not very nice." Little girls of five are unfamiliar with the term "clitoris" and are more than likely to state that the "vagina" is dirty.

Although rare at age three, by age five there are already distortions and conflicts of the sex drive. A few children compulsively but joylessly masturbate in ways that invite discovery and parental displeasure. Others request enemas and suppositories for the sensations they impart. Some little boys seek out and oblige older homosexuals, without seeming to derive any pleasure from the contact. Sprouting eroticism is easily damaged and difficult to restore.

Once past this most difficult age, normal children begin to expand their erotic horizons once more, in ways calculated to avoid discovery. Children over seven are well aware of adult attitudes about sex. They devise elaborate strategies to present themselves as innocent. Foreplay and orgasms are achieved in cellars, haylofts, and attics. Those who have temporarily abstained from masturbation often begin again. The accumulative incidence of masturbation in boys rises from ten percent at age seven to eighty percent at age thirteen. Heterosexual play rises from less than five percent at age five, to a third at age eight, and two thirds at age thirteen. (Ramsey, 1943)

A steadily increasing minority of boys are engaged in coitus. Orgasms without ejaculation do occur. There is no rest necessary following orgasm, so that serial climaxes crop up in quick succession. Girls, who begin life with a greater erotic response, continue to lag far behind, although their trend is similar.

In early puberty the divergence between the sexes becomes even more striking. The adolescent boy has his eroticism imposed by nature. There is an enormous rise in the erotogenic hormone, testosterone, which can produce intense sexual interest when administered to either sex. Nocturnal orgasms occur without encouragement or permission. The penis rubs against clothing and immediately responds to the sight or thought of an amenable maiden. The boy has fewer constraints and may be subtly encouraged by his father and openly urged by schoolmates. Older brothers may provide instruction. In contrast, the girl experiences a rise in the female hormones, estrogen and progesterone. These contribute little to her eroticism, and may even detract from it. She may still be unaware of her clitoris, which is tucked away beneath several fleshy folds and unromantically named "down there." Confusion and anxiety may accompany the onset of menses, the presence of blood, and often some discomfort. She is never to appreciate the raw, unsolicited gratification of a wet dream. She is beset by cultural remonstrances, ignorance, shame, and the fear of gossip. Most importantly, she has a past marked by deficiencies in erotic pleasure.

Kinsey states:

> Fifty percent of the girls from the upper social levels manage to arrive at marriage before they have ever experienced sexual arousal to the point of complete climax. Many people are proud of this, and think it an ideal which the boy might very well follow. But the girl has achieved her so-called sublimation as a result of a long build-up of inhibitions. Against her record of no orgasms before marriage, the male she weds has a record of some thousand or fifteen hundred climaxes. One hardly needs to look further for the chief cause of sexual incompatibilities in marriage. One-half of all these previously unresponsive girls—that is one quarter to a third of all the women who marry—will fail to come to climax in intercourse after marriage.

In 1970, Masters and Johnson estimate that half of all marriages are sexually dysfunctional. Others, such as Waggoner (1974), feel that this is a conservative estimate. It is generally agreed that women are far more impaired than men, and that this is related to their lack of early sex experience. The overwhelming preponderance of orgasmic dysfunction in women is clearly related to their lack of early sex experience.

Although the young male commonly attains a climax efficiently, he is beset by other problems. He ruminates about the size of his penis, the persistence of his erection, or his ability to satisfy his mate. He experiences a pervasive sense of inadequacy which transforms the bed into an arena or, occasionally, a dunce stool. His anxiety precipitates premature ejaculation, retarded ejaculation, and impotence. His problems also emanate from childhood, especially from sexually blurred and unenthusiastic parenting. Fifty percent of all marriages are estimated to suffer from some form of sexual dysfunction. Sex clinics are manifesting an unprecedented expansion. Training programs for therapists are full, and couples who need treatment are placed on long waiting lists. Those who request aid are but a tiny fraction of those who could benefit. Some who request treatment cannot be helped.

How can we prevent this misery? The only possible prevention lies in the development of a positive, enthusiastic approach to children's sexuality. The roots of all dysfunctions extend back to early childhood, and even in the first year of their lives, we shape our children's capacity for pleasure. The sex drive is singularly vulnerable. It can be diverted, elaborated, constricted, or squelched. We need to understand and nourish the wellsprings of eroticism.

We have entered an exciting era of sexual enrichment. With Alex Comfort at bedside, we massage each other's feet, communicate fantasies, and abandon deodorants. Erotic art, once confined to San Francisco's North Beach, or Amsterdam's sex shops, is available at the corner newsstand. Yet we who frolic on the satin sheets of youth are strangely reticent with progeny.

Even the perception of the eager suckling infant is eclipsed by the need to deny erotic import. He is "cute," or "famished," but never passionate. Nursing is reduced to such aseptic components as calories and formulas. To nurse or not is a decision for or against an intensely erotic experience. Some mothers are rendered embarrassed and anxious by their own response. The nipple comes erect and hardens at the infant's eager approach. Seconds later the breast tingles as the milk spurts forcefully. The rhythmic tugging at the nipple elicits genital sensations. Some women experience serial orgasms, and then drift into a refreshing slumber.

Fewer than twenty percent of mothers in the United States today nurse their infants. Many of those offer the breast as a duty, and soon abandon the effort. Very few are able simply and quietly to offer the teat and savor the sensations.

Those who choose not to nurse give reasons with which a good Victorian could have rationalized sexual abstinence. Breast-feeding is dirty, messy, embarrassing, and inconvenient. It can wreck mother's body, sag her appendages, derail her from productive efforts, sap her strength, and keep her from knowing how much milk her infant is getting. Nursing may make infants hard to wean because they like it too much. They may get too full, not receive their vitamins, or waste away. The central values are production, cleanliness, appearance, and the scientific method. Mutual pleasuring between mother and infant is conspicuously absent. In fact, the mother is thought to experience more pleasure if she doesn't nurse, for lactation will tie her down and make her less sexually attractive.

The woman who chooses to nurse in spite of these discomforts has at her command many strategies and appliances to ward off pleasure. She can allow her infant to suck only for specified periods through the porthole of her triply reinforced nursing bra. Though weary, she may sit upright, evacuating her teat at the infant's first sign of satiation. A relief bottle allows her to "rest." If still queasy at the infant's raw excitement, the uncontrolled squirting of the milk, and the moistened underwear, she soon begins to prefer the sterile bottle.

As we shall see, the skin-to-skin contact between mother and infant constitutes the basic erotic experience. These sensations also contribute to the most fundamental form of intimacy—body intimacy.

My mother was young and liberated in the 1920's. She attended college, and studied as the only female in the department of anthropology of the graduate school at Harvard. She traveled to Europe, smoked, and drank. She had several affairs before she married my father. My father had been raised in a strict, prohibitionist family, where on Sunday children were permitted only to read the Bible. He was entranced by my liberated mother. Both my mother and father allowed me to see them naked and to join that bare expanse of skin beneath the covers on a Sunday morning. Recalling such earthy license, I was astonished years later to hear that my mother often refused my father sex. Her record for rejection was three years while in her thirties.

When my mother bathed me, she reserved the genital area until last. She scrubbed it harshly, indicating that I had better learn to wipe myself clean with the toilet tissue. When old enough to bathe myself, I avoided washing or touching that tainted area. At age five I contracted a vaginal infection. My mother took me to a gynecologist without assessing the problem herself. The doctor gingerly examined me while my mother commented on the stench. He recommended sitz baths. Night after night I sat for a half hour in three inches of tepid water well laced with boric acid. I thought my foulness would contaminate the water and cause a rash. I felt dirtier after bathing than before. The infection cleared up faster than my fantasies.

By the time I entered medical school, I was married and had borne two children. I still avoided tub baths and scrubbed hastily in the shower. I had never masturbated, climaxed, nor viewed my sexual organs in the mirror. I might have waited for Alex Comfort with the other unfortunates of my overactive but undersexed generation, had it not been for freshman anatomy. My cadaver was a female. I ruminated upon my own naïveté as I dissected her shriveled organs through the acrid fumes of formaldehyde. With scientific fervor I promised to investigate not only my anatomy, but my sexual function as well. With Grant's *Atlas of Anatomy* propped at bedside, I began my task.

The years that followed were crowded by work and children, carefully reared according to Dr. Spock. Above all, I avoided my mother's mistakes with my own offspring and made no connection between genitals and dirt. I didn't think my children had sexual problems. Indeed, there was little or no ostensible erotic activity, for which I was mildly thankful. One little girl did develop a passionate interest in playing "horsey." She wrapped her legs about my body and ecstatically rubbed her pubis up and down. Too sophisticated to push her away, I calmly but firmly placed her aside and rose to cook dinner. I refused to play "horsey" again.

My oldest daughters are now in their twenties. Separately, each has confided concern about an incomplete erotic response. How could this be? Didn't I read the right books? Hadn't I avoided the pitfalls of my own childhood? Belatedly, I realized that I had never said anything nice about sex. I had averted my eyes, studied my replies, hushed my husband's moans of pleasure, and locked the bedroom door.

Three generations had repeated.

2

PARENTING PAPERBACKS

UNFORTUNATELY, SEXUAL AND OTHER REVOLUTIONS ARE A LOT
of work with rather prosaic returns. The most that our generation can accomplish is a gradual disengagement from the
misconceptions of our time. Our past remains to permeate
the present. One less-than-liberated woman asks her physician if it is true that homosexual children result from the
rear-entry coital position. Another inquires if it's wrong for
her sixty-five-year-old husband still to want sex. An adolescent
boy asks his coach if there is any way to prevent the wet
dreams that impair his athletic prowess.

Each generation advances intellectually, but lags emotionally. A medical student and his young wife are able to
speak about sex with his mother, a just-liberated matron.
The young couple tests the depth of the mother's newfound
philosophy by discussing many intimate details. The mother
doesn't even blush. She replies with a shady joke and a sex
manual quotation of her own. Finally, the young wife describes the intricate manipulations necessary for her vagina
to lubricate. She suddenly turns and asks her mother-in-law,
"What does it take for *you* to get juiced up, Mom?" The
mother blushes, stammers, and is unable to answer.

Attitudes toward childhood masturbation have aptly illustrated changes in our attitudes toward sex. Prior to the
eighteenth century, masturbation was condemned solely on

moral grounds. Thereafter, the habit became inexorably wedded to physical disease. Masturbation was said to cause insanity, tuberculosis, syphilis, eventual impotence, or sterility, and deformed children. Those unable to control their urges sometimes committed sucide in despair. Any indulgence was the forerunner of fatal addiction.

Treatment was so drastic as to seem macabre. One physician recommended that the clitoris be "freely excised either by scissors or knife—I always prefer the scissors." The nerves leading to the penis were cut, an operation which produced permanent impotence. This was a small price to pay for freedom from debilitating disease. (Baker, 1866) In fact, one disease was created in order to explain nocturnal emissions or "wet dreams." This disease, "spermatorrhea," connoted intrinsic evil and was a penalty for early, heavy masturbation. (Schwartz, 1973)

In 1854, Charles Drysdale presented the following ominous account of this condition:

> The victim wakes suddenly from a stupor, just as the discharge is pouring out, which he will try in vain to check; or perhaps he does not wake till it is over, and then, as a lethargic consciousness, which of itself tells him what has taken place, slowly awakens, he puts down his hand and sickens with despair, as he perceives the fatal drain, and thinks on the gloomy morrow which will follow. . . . The patient may, after years of suffering, sink into the lowest stage of weakness, and die . . . the disease has in many cases progressed to insanity, and idiocy . . .

Gerhart Schwartz describes the profusion of mechanical devices to correct spermatorrhea which flooded an eager market. Most were spike-lined rings, to be placed about the penis at bedtime. Uncomfortable, but not unbearable without an erection, they produced excruciating pain when the penis distended. This immediately awakened the unfortunate wretch, who was then told to take a cold bath in order to relieve his excitation. Electric shocks and tight bandages were also employed. In 1908, Miss Perkins, a nurse who worked in a sanitarium, wrote about the most secure and complete device to prevent masturbation. She called it "Sexual Armour":

> It is a deplorable but well-known fact that one of the most common causes of insanity, imbecility and feeble-mindedness, especially in youth, is due to masturbation or self-abuse. This is about equally true of both sexes. Physicians, nurses and attendants associated with insane asylums have long found this habit the most difficult of all bad practices to eradicate, because of the incessant attention required of them in respect to the subjects in their care. . . . Therefore, with persons who have carried on such disastrous practices until serious ailments of the mind have resulted, there has been but little hope of cure. . . .
>
> My profession has made me very familiar with this subject and the many melancholy human tragedies of this character which have transpired before my own eyes have impressed upon me the great necessity of a device which will aid those concerned in the treatment of such cases, and the cure from this disastrous practice, and which will at the same time give the person under treatment all necessary personal liberty.

Her contraption consisted of a steel and leather jacket which enveloped the entire lower torso. Perforations allowed urine to escape. A hinged trap-door, bolted and padlocked in back, was opened by a second individual in order to allow for defecation. Other such devices were sold accompanied by handcuffs for additional protection.

About the turn of the century, a Michigan physician described his patient, a girl of seven:

> She had been taught the habit by vicious children, at a country house from which she was adopted in the summer of 1895. I learned from the foster mother that on the advice of physicians she had given her worm remedies, they thinking that, perhaps, the irritation was due to the migration of pinworms. The parts had been kept thoroughly cleansed; she had

been made to sleep in sheep-skin pants and jackets made into one garment with her hands tied to a collar about her neck; her feet were tied to the foot-board and by a strap about her waist she was fastened to the head-board so that she couldn't slide down in bed and use her heels; she had been reasoned with, scolded, and whipped, and in spite of it all she managed to keep up the habit.

This benevolent physician snipped and cleansed the tissue, thinking that the problem was due to irritation from infection. The first night after the operation, she tore off the dressings, opened up the wound with her fingers, and bled profusely. (Schwartz, 1973)

Although we often think of the United States as more advanced than its conservative European counterparts, concern with masturbation declined more slowly here. After World War I, supply houses still carried sexual restraints in their catalogues. Medical textbooks continued to mention mechanical devices, but noted their relative ineffectiveness in other than small children. As late as the 1970's a well-known textbook in urology mentioned several unfavorable conditions caused by self-manipulation.

Dr. Martha Wolfenstein has traced changes in attitude toward masturbation through her analysis of the publications of the United States Children's Bureau. Through the years these pamphlets have presented the accepted standards of child rearing. (Wolfenstein, 1953)

Between 1914 and 1921, the danger of children's sexuality was painfully evident. If not promptly and rigorously squelched, both thumb-sucking and masturbation would permanently damage the child. The prescribed treatment was to bind the hands and feet, the body spread-eagled on the bed, so that the child could not suck his thumb, touch the genitals, or even rub thighs together. Total eradication of any self-pleasuring was the goal of responsible parents.

In 1929, the focus of severity shifted to early rigorous bowel training, and exact feeding schedules. For the first time, milder methods were recommended for the control of masturbation. A baby could be given a toy to divert his attention.

In 1938, masturbation was presented as normal exploration, of little consequence. Sexuality was no longer seen as crippling and dangerous, but rather as an unimportant incident, often embarrassing to the mother. In contrast, thumb-sucking still required mechanical restraint.

The trend toward leniency continued. In 1951, mothers were told that masturbation does not amount to anything, although children sometimes touch their genitals while on the toilet. The mother may experience uncomfortable feelings when she observes this, and for her own sake can distract the child with a toy.

For years parents have accepted this dogma without question. Yet what message does this attitude of studied indifference or anxious distraction give the child? Young children are not stupid. The toddler accurately senses the mother's mood. The message he receives is a message of apprehension or disapproval.

Most parents validate children's positive behavior. They say, "Your hair is so pretty the way you brushed it" or "You can be proud of making your bed so well." These messages are clear and not subject to misinterpretation. Teachers use the same approach to reinforce good behavior at school.

No one reinforces children's sexuality. We actively avoid mentioning or observing it. Have you ever heard a mother say to a child found fondling himself: "My, you've really learned how to make yourself feel good." Or have you heard a father say to his son: "It's real nice that your penis is getting bigger"? Instead, children are confronted with anxiety and ambivalence.

Today a visit to the local bookstore reveals shelf upon shelf of parenting paperbacks. The only rival in quantity is the section on sex. The big names in parenting are there: Spock, Ginott, and even some authors, such as Stella Chess, who have published extensively in the professional literature. In a surprising number, neither masturbation nor sex is listed in the index. This is especially so in books about the Montessori method. This method suggests that children who are well occupied manipulating objects should never need to manipulate themselves. Young minds are more profitably directed toward academic pursuits, and eroticism constitutes an uneconomical pastime. Is this again the "fatal drain"?

Most prominently on the shelf in the bookstore is Dr. Benjamin Spock's time-tested *Baby and Child Care*. This has been the parent's bible for two generations. The near-perfect face of a white infant still smiles merrily from the cover in spite of heightened racial consciousness.

Well recognized for his scope and common sense, Spock devotes four and one half pages to the subject of masturbation in each of the 1968 and 1976 revisions. He states: "We were all brought up to be disturbed by it, and we can never unlearn that. . . . It's quite appropriate when a mother discovers a child in sex play to give him the idea that she doesn't want him to do it anymore, in a tone that implies that this will help him to stop." In 1976, Spock advocates an individual approach and speaks of his own concern for the neighbors' disapproval. Mothers can remonstrate mildly, "It isn't polite," or "Most fathers and mothers don't want their children to play this way," or "I don't like to see you doing it," or "That kind of play is for grownups, not for children." He indicates that shooing a child out to some other activity is usually enough to stop sex play for a long time in a *normal* * child.

In both editions he describes the toddler's interest in sex as a wholesome but transient curiosity. A fifteen-month-old girl, sitting on the potty, may explore herself for a few seconds at a time. Distracting the child with a toy is permissible but not always necessary.

* Italics mine.

Between three and six, children are described as having true sexual feelings, rather than just curiosity. The clearly comprehensible Spock is suddenly murky. We learn that frequent or excessive masturbation is a serious condition. A sign of tenseness or worry, it may be "due to something else going wrong in the child's life or spirit." Rapid assess· ment, perhaps involving a child psychiatrist, is indicated. But Spock does not define "excessive." It must be more than the few seconds at a time attributed to the toddler's wholesome curiosity! In order to explain "excessive," Spock gives several examples. One is an eight-year-old boy, terrified that his mother might die, who absently handles his genitals in school while gazing out the window. Another is an almost three-year-old boy who views his infant sister's lack of penis and begins to hold his own appendage anxiously. These "excessive" masturbators seem neither very active nor very interested. Masturbation is presented as an altogether uncomfortable, but perhaps necessary, part of development which usually warrants distraction or mild suppression. Never is masturbation primarily pleasurable or desirable.

Spock is a moderate. He warns against telling children that masturbation will injure their genitals, or that it leads to insanity. Yet he suggests that more than a vaguely defined amount is a danger signal. It can proclaim a serious emotional problem. Are serious emotional problems so different from the older concept of insanity? He feels that it is quite proper for parents to uphold society's disapproval of sexuality if they agree with society. He doesn't offer instructions to those who disagree with society.

Most enlightening is Spock's recent account of his own early life published in a collection of various celebrities' first sexual experiences. Spock recounts a childhood dominated by a moralistic and opinionated mother who never, ever, changed her mind. Spock, as the oldest of six, is the chief target of her prohibitions. His mother cites sex as sinful and threatens that if a child touches himself he will have deformed offspring. Spock associates with some strange bedfellows in *The First Time*. Such raw and brassy collaborators as Mae West and Erica Jong disgorge spectacular details of their first sexual experiences. Not so Spock—with dignity, he circumvents any salacious material. Spock's "first time" is never depicted. Dr. Benjamin Spock is a compassionate pediatrician and a magnificent gentleman. He's as human as the rest of us.

More fashionable but less durable than Spock is Dr. Haim G. Ginott. He devotes only two pages to the topic of masturbation in his book *Between Parent and Child*. Far more negative than Spock, he makes the following statements:

> Intellectually, parents recognize that masturbation may be a phase in the development of normal sexuality. Emotionally, it is hard to accept. And perhaps parents are not altogether wrong in not sanctioning masturbation.
>
> Self-gratification may make the child less accessible to the influence of his parents and peers. When he takes the shortcut to gratification, he does not have to depend on pleasing anyone but himself . . .
>
> Parents may exert a mild pressure against self-indulgence, not because it is pathological, but because it is not progressive; it does not result in social relationships or personal growth. The pressure must be mild or it will back-fire in wild explosions.

Ginott presents masturbation as a siphoning off of vital energies which could better be devoted to accomplishments in behalf of self and society. This is again reminiscent of Drysdale's "fatal drain." One pictures the masturbating child floating directionless in a sea of marshmallows, while his personality disintegrates. Ginott's title to the section on masturbation is "Self-gratification or Self-abuse?" One concludes that masturbation is self-abuse.

And what are the "wild explosions" that may result from indelicate management? We must treat sexual matters cautiously lest there be an eruption. The monster within must not be provoked. Sexuality, then, is also a monster.

Several other books present masturbation as a necessary part of the learning process, implying that pleasure is secondary or absent. These texts stress that any continued interest in touching denotes anxiety. Further investigation, possible psychotherapy, or restrictions are warranted. Dorothy Corkville Briggs, in a psychologically sophisticated volume entitled *Your Child's Self Esteem,* states that one cannot prevent the child's initial discovery of the penis, but she reassures the reader that anyway this is different from the adult experience.

In *Your Child is a Person* by Stella Chess and Thomas Birch, masturbation is presented as an accidental discovery requiring casual treatment and distinct directives such as, "People don't do that in public."

Dr. Lee Salk, in *What Every Child Would Like His Parents to Know,* continues this theme of casual treatment. One should "let him know that you know, but ignore the situation as much as possible." If masturbation seems frequent or excessive, one might make such statements as "If you want to do what you are doing, why don't you go off and do it by yourself?" "I guess it feels good, but why do you do it so often?" He also indicates that children have a secret hope that someone will set limits on what is socially acceptable.

Dr. Fitzhugh Dodson is billed as a successor to both Dr. Spock and Dr. Ginott. In Dodson's book, *How to Parent,* he makes a most remarkable statement: "To a toddler, his penis is no more inherently interesting than his finger or his toes." This theme of equivalency is continued as he recommends a positive approach to teaching a boy the word "penis" by pointing or touching in sequence just as one would teach a child to identify his ears or nose. He doesn't cover how to teach the words "clitoris" or "vagina" to little girls.

The popular books on parenting present consistent and culturally acceptable views of children's sexuality. The sexy child remains a threat to parental self-esteem by evoking fears of loss of control or moral disintegration. The authors recommend that we overlook, disapprove of, or correct eroticism in children. A few, caught in the midst of cultural dissonance, devalue sex or relate it to learning rather than feeling. Thus it is necessary but never nice. The child contends with absent, ambiguous, or negative responses from his parents. He quickly senses their anxiety and need for constraint. He correctly interprets sex as a distressing or cumbersome area.

How can we align these views of sexuality with the adult inclination toward increasing depth and richness of the sexual experience? Small wonder that the sex clinics continue their exponential expansion. We shall feed them patients in the future by continuing to inhibit and distort the sexual drives in our children. Nowhere is the need for prevention as great. Yet parents, in their misguided search for the proper approach, continue to saddle children with vestiges of the Victorian ethic.

In the last century we have progressed from picturing the erotic child as a diseased pervert to seeing him or her as a behavioral problem demanding considered restraint. Some parents are now able to tolerate, but not enjoy, some sexual expression, especially if they don't have to view it.

As a culture we remain preoccupied with penis size and penis envy. When will we begin systematically to develop penis pride in our boys and feelings of clitoral worth in our girls?

3

CHALLENGE TO CHANGE

IF SEXUAL EXPERIENCES PRODUCE CHILDREN WITH A HEALTHY and direct interest in sex, what do we as parents have to fear? Our fears are as prolific as our fantasies. The monster of sexual pleasure, once loosed, might no longer be controllable. Children would experiment together sexually on the front porch, or rape and incest would become common. Imagine if you will a trip to the supermarket with your small sexy child. How embarrassing to find him with one hand stroking a melon and the other in his pants!

We as parents try much harder not to do wrong than to do right. It is for the visionary or the activist to explore new paths. By the time we assume the massive responsibility of parenthood, we attempt only to navigate the middle of a well-worn road.

The fear that we may lose control of our children's impulses is part of our fear that we may lose control of our own. If we expressed our sexual desires freely, would there ever be time for work? What would our parents say? Would supper be ready on time? Our intent to live productive, sensible lives ever reinforces our need to control ourselves and our children.

Our children seem like an especially visible and often unpredictable part of our souls. We expect that people will judge us by our offspring. The mother on the subway who glances down to find her little girl rubbing the leg of her doll against her crotch is mortified, turns scarlet, and pushes her small charge off the train onto the platform at the next station.

A more difficult, if less visible, area is the child who approaches an adult with obvious sexual interest. A four-year-old girl squarely demands to see and feel the bulge beneath her father's zipper. A five-year-old boy, afraid of the dark, climbs in bed with his mother and later rubs against her bare posterior. Parents are confused and upset.

When does the intimacy of infancy cease? It is permissible, after all, to allow the suckling eight-month-old infant absently to finger the mother's other nipple? When does the needy, innocent infant become a threat to the parent's sense of morality? This depends upon the mother's comfort with her own sexuality. If we fear the monster within, then we dread the monster in our child.

What can we as parents do with these fears? Many of us will recognize the problem but elect to do nothing. There's safety in sameness—sex is a loaded subject which could backfire. In spite of this, some parents will painfully reflect upon their own erotic limitations, wishing that they had been raised with more open acceptance or even encouragement of sexuality. What then can they do to facilitate a more robust and joyful response for their children? How do they avoid the pitfalls and how far is far enough? The answers can be appreciated through an understanding of the child's erotic development.

The infant is born with a tremendous erotic potential. If this is realized, he or she will become a fully orgasmic adult. The sexual experience will be intensely gratifying, largely predictable, and persistent even into old age. But the newborn infant doesn't know what sex is or how to do it—or much else, for that matter. Erotic gratification begins as a diffuse sensation involving the whole body. He feels sexy in much the same way he feels hungry—all over. He's either satiated and asleep or screaming with frustration. As his mother picks him up, cuddles and feeds him, he becomes acquainted with warmth, the mother's scent, sweetness in his mouth, and pressure on his genitals. His bowels stop grumbling and his penis may erect. He's learning what feels good. Eventually he will seek these pleasures. At five months he squirms and wriggles with excitement as the breast approaches. He grasps it fiercely with both fists and sucks vigorously. He has established a drive—for hunger, sex, and closeness. All three blend and mingle as one. At eight months the infant distinguishes between various forms of pleasure. He can do many things for himself, such as eat toast without his mother's help or feel his genitals if he is so inclined. This ability to do different things at different times aids in separating one drive from another. Even so, countless interrelations between the need for food, warmth, and erotic sensations persist into adult life. An intimate conversation in front of a fire is a fine aphrodisiac at any age.

There is another extremely significant change during the first year which affects erotic expression during the entire life span. The child forms a meaningful relationship with his mother or whoever is his primary caretaker. This doesn't occur in the first half year because then the infant has only the dimmest perception of his environment. He's far more concerned with inner tensions than the outer world. If his tummy is full and his intestines placid, he's more than likely asleep. His mother contributes to the pleasantness of his emotional climate simply by heeding his cues and predictably providing him with a spectrum of gratifications as she rocks, soothes, and changes him. Recently researchers have discovered that even newborns can recognize the mother. Yet for months the mother exists as an evanescent extension of the baby's neediness rather than as a separate individual. When he cries, his mother appears like a genie to do his bidding; when he's comfortable, he pays her scant attention. He accepts a strange baby-sitter with equanimity—providing his needs are quickly met. In the second six months the child sees his mother as a separate person. He realizes that she responds not only to his command but to other pressures as well. His self-esteem suffers; his mother is not his servant. He's been demoted from general to recruit. If the mother leaves him with another person his world crumbles; he whimpers, sucks his thumb, and petulantly refuses the kindest offerings. Now the relationship with his mother is a reciprocal, highly charged, and all-encompassing commitment. He's acutely aware of her mood and attitude, for she is his first sweetheart. If his mother is happy or sad, he will know it. If she avoids looking at or touching his penis, he will know that too.

It's within this essential relationship that *body intimacy* develops. Body intimacy is a physical and emotional link which forms between the needy, dependent infant and his loving mother. It is predicated upon the early, eager, joyful inclusion of another warm, responsive being—without reservation or contingency. Highly erotic, this bond is the foundation for all later intimacies. The mother's emotional state is crucial during the construction of this link, for the child must find himself mirrored in his mother's eyes. (Winnecott, 1971) If her response is eager and joyful, the infant views himself as valuable. He also derives a sense of goodness or badness from her reactions. If she babbles and smiles except when she changes his diaper, he soon understands that a certain part of his body is less acceptable than the rest.

In 1945, René Spitz demonstrated the importance of the early emotional climate when he described the infants in a hygienic but emotionally barren foundling home. There, babies were left in cribs when they were not being changed or fed. Passive and listless, they showed little curiosity or appetite. They distrusted even the most charitable adult and preferred to stay alone. They remained scrawny, dull, and vacant children. One might expect that such empty youngsters would turn to their own bodies as a source of comfort. In fact, they seemed far less intrigued by genital pleasures than did normal infants. They rocked back and forth on hands and knees, banged their heads painfully again and again, pulled their hair out by the roots, and chewed on the metal crib. Appetite was erratic, growth was stunted, and strange food preferences were common.

Thanks to Frederick Leboyer and others, we now begin to appreciate the extensive impact of the early years. A characteristic temperament is discernible in the first half year, and a style of relatedness in the second half. These factors continue to influence emotional and sexual growth at later ages. Just how does this come about? It occurs because the child forms a set of prophecies based on his earliest experiences. He expects that adults will respond to him in a certain way—always loving, sometimes scary, or generally resentful. He proceeds to act in a manner which causes his predictions to come true. For instance, children who have suffered severe beatings and then are placed in foster homes are quite often cruel to pets, destroy furniture, and blatantly disobey the foster parents. It's as if they ask to be beaten. Children can relearn more favorable patterns of relatedness, but only if the environment responds differently than they expect.

Sexual behavior is governed by the same principles. The little girl who has noted that her mother turns away or appears upset when she fingers her genitals concludes that her genitals are bad and that others will dislike them also. She can relearn a more positive attitude only if she has experiences which affirm her sexual organs as good—and there are precious few of these available. With other problems such as a lagging appetite, there are a thousand corrective experiences available, like Thanksgiving at Grandma's or making her own peanut butter "sammich" after school. When negative attitudes and expectations persist over the years, they become firmly entrenched.

A few youngsters do retain the open curiosity and robust humor of healthy sexuality. They owe their escape to rather remarkable parents who have encouraged and skillfully guided them. The following examples illustrate these fortunate children.

MICHAEL

A young university couple wished to limit their family to two children. The firstborn boy, Walter, was raised according to child-development manuals and Dr. Ginott. The grandmother's helpful hints to the contrary were politely deflected, as the couple felt that it was their responsibility to raise their children better than they had been raised. Consequently, Walter was weaned from the breast at six months and not toilet-trained until two years. He was provided with Playskool toys and books which were read to him at bedtime. He knew the colors and could print his name at age four. When Walter entered nursery school he was a tractable child who obeyed rules and liked to learn. In the children's bathroom at nursery school, Walter forgot his own urinary pressures while watching the girls. He seemed startled when teacher gently reminded him that he was there for a purpose.

When Walter was four years old, an infant brother, Michael, was born. By that time the family was well established, and the mother felt competent and secure as a parent. She read fewer books and spent more time holding, nuzzling, and playing games with Michael. She reluctantly weaned him at nine and a half months because she knew that longer suckling was unusual. Realizing that this was her last infant, she indulged him fully. The father was less demanding with Michael than he had been with Walter. He read and wrestled with both boys.

At the nursery school, Michael was described as likable, with a good sense of humor. One teacher tended to favor Michael and sometimes gave him more attention than the other children. Michael enjoyed the community bathroom and often persuaded two little girls to watch him urinate.

Walter is now almost seventeen and Michael thirteen. Walter has begun to date now that he has a part-time job and some money saved. He is anxious about girls and asks his parents many questions. He plans to attend a large state university next year. Michael is less organized but more enthusiastic than his brother. His grades are good although he seldom studies except before a test. Girls in his class call him frequently on the telephone and he loves it. Although he has never been on a formal date, he is most often in the company of the opposite sex.

Recently Walter informed his mother that Michael was reading "dirty books." His mother, already aware of some salacious material in Michael's underwear drawer, asked Walter what he thought was "dirty." Walter intimated that Michael was spending several hours each afternoon reading *Everything You Always Wanted to Know About Sex*. His mother, with a twinkle in her eye, corralled and confronted Michael, who readily admitted to his research. He snickered and said, "It's not going to be any of that three-minute stuff for me!" Mother was convulsed with laughter. Michael was an unlikely candidate for sex therapy.

Like many a firstborn child, Walter was the more constrained and responsible of the children. Yet his parents never consciously inhibited Walter. They did persistently emphasize the value of achievement; work came first. Body intimacies such as hugging and sitting close were secondary to learning the correct answer and behaving properly. Achievement and good behavior were also emphasized with Michael, but were balanced by the mutual enjoyment of body warmth and closeness.

PAULA

Paula was the only girl in a family of seven children. Both parents and a host of relatives were delighted with her arrival. She was showered with lacy dresses and pink booties. Although the father had taken part in caring for all the infants, he enjoyed Paula even more. As soon as Paula walked she would go from lap to lap soliciting tickles and cuddling with each family member. When relatives gathered she was the center of attention. Parents were not upset when at the tender age of three she presented herself naked in front of company. Her father laughed and tapped her derriere as she ran giggling back to the bedroom. When Paula was five years old she was not as responsible as her brothers had been at that age. Recognizing this, her father refused to cuddle her unless she helped her mother set the table. Several times he was irritated when she left her tricycle in the street or dropped her candy wrappers on the floor. Paula ran to her mother, and her mother marched her back to her father, who spoke sternly to her. When Paula entered school, teachers described her as "immature." She would stand and wail if someone took her swing, and she had no friends who played with her. The parents observed that after school Paula's brothers would rush to her assistance whenever she cried. They chased away bigger and more aggressive children. The parents called a family conference where Paula's problems were discussed and certain goals determined. Mother began to check with care under the bed and behind the bureau where Paula had stuffed dirty clothes. Her brothers ceased responding to her tears and her father began to supervise homework closely. By the end of the first grade, other children liked to play with Paula and the teacher described her as "cute and smart."

At the age of eight Paula played an intriguing game called "Truth, Dare, or Consequences" in a neighborhood clubhouse. Paula dared a friend to streak naked around a house. One "consequence" was for Paula to show her "pee-hole." One of Paula's older brothers heard about these activities and told his parents. Her mother thought it wasn't nice and should be stopped before it caused a furor in the neighborhood. The father reminded her that they had both had such experiences when young and advised her to forget it. Instead of interrupting the games, the mother provided Paula with sex education books written for children.

Paula did well in school and continued to college. She

astutely chose boyfriends who were considerate of her but successful in their own right. After college graduation she developed her own public relations firm. By the age of twenty-five she was already well established, employing five men and two women. Her workers felt Paula was both competent and sensitive to their problems. Paula initiated several long-term relationships with different men. At the age of twenty-eight she decided to marry a corporation executive with a similar background. After five years of marriage she described herself as happy, intentionally childless, and sexually fulfilled.

That Paula was both aggressive and sexually responsive is no accident. In bed and at the office she asks for what she wants, without shame or fear of rejection. This ability to take risks is a prime therapy goal of the sex clinics. The woman who expects that her partner will automatically know her needs must feel resentful when he fails. She remains inert, patiently waiting, and still too embarrassed and frightened to ask. Finally she gives up and passively accepts the crumbs from the banquet. On the other hand, the sexually aggressive woman frees her mate from the responsibility of masterminding her orgasm and actively reassures him of his virility and expertise. Assertion can also provide the woman with other important benefits. The aggressive girl is better adjusted, less likely to suffer emotional disorders, develops a higher IQ, and attains greater achievement.

How can we train girls in healthy assertion? First, we need mothers who are themselves active and fulfilled and who can ask for what they want. The overburdened and unenthusiastic "trapped young mother" presents a blurred, listless model for her daughter. We need fathers who not only tolerate, but delight in their daughter's assertion. We need both parents to nurture little girls less. (Baumarind, 1972) For example, when Melinda tearfully complains that Johnny hit her, mother rocks and comforts her. Father looks for Johnny in order to "set things straight." Melinda is being programmed for docility and immaturity. Her parents appear clairvoyant because they always seem to know and satisfy her needs. She doesn't need to stand up to adversaries, compete, plan for the future, or ask for what she wants.

CHILDREN OF THE FARM COMMUNE

Some years ago, I met a graduate student in psychology who lived in a farm commune in northern California. Eight to twelve adults shared the labor of a 120-acre dairy farm. More than half the grownups were also involved in higher level studies, and several were artists. Duties were apportioned according to skill, interest, and need. One adult was assigned to care for the three or four infants and toddlers. Older children attended a nearby public school, although an effort was made to extend their education at home. Organization and planning were discussed at a weekly house meeting.

The key philosophy was to share whenever possible, with little distinction between adults and children. Children shared wine at dinner, were included when a joint was passed, and were asked their opinion on important matters. Children's activities were seldom restricted. When not studying or helping, they ran freely through the barn and fields. As soon as they were old enough to walk a distance or carry a load they were assigned chores which were a meaningful and necessary part of the farm existence. Thus a four-year-old was seen clasping with both arms a measure of hay much larger than she was in order to feed the cow. Two adults who liked children collected an entourage resembling the Pied Piper's. It was difficult to match children with their parents, since any grownup could instruct or nurture any child. Occasionally a mother and her children, or a family unit, would depart because of incompatability or other interests. Children grieved openly when the departure entailed the loss of a valued friend.

Although the farmhouse was large, it was scarcely capacious enough. Children roomed with adults, sometimes in sleeping bags on the floor. Sexual activities were not only observed but openly discussed. In the morning, children would portray the last night's drama in a squirmy, giggling heap, to the amusement of the adults.

Not only were the children exposed to the sights and sounds of adult intercourse, but they also observed chickens, dogs, and sheep. Copulation between favorite animals was a continued subject of avid interest. When the cow was taken to be bred, six children accompanied the expedition to observe and comment on the bull's awesome organ. Later the children played out the scene in graphic detail in a game called "Bang Bossie." Both boys and girls competed for the favored role of bull but enjoyed the cow's position also. Passing adults smiled or offered a humorous comment. Children under four were never restrained from touching the breasts of a lactating mother. Older children were deterred by remarks such as "See? He still thinks he's a tit-baby." As children grew, chores became more difficult. The time devoted to sex play was necessarily curtailed, but never absent.

During my many visits to the commune I spent time with the children. As a group they seemed independent and sexually astute. They appreciated social nuances and effectively asserted themselves in meetings. I observed no irrational fears, no exaggerated dependencies, and no disregard for the feelings of others. These children were confident, cooperative, and never arrogant. By the age of eight they were restrained about sexual matters outside the commune. They betrayed their sophistication by a whispered remark or a mischievous grin.

This unusual background will continue to distinguish these children in the future. They may not attain the educational achievements of their parents and may have problems adapting to the more conventional middle-class culture. However, I am certain that the immense erotic enrichment prior to puberty will serve as protective armor against later sexual dysfunctions. Melting erections and absent climaxes are unlikely where erotic play and orgasms have become a way of life.

GRACE

Grace was the first of six children born to an immigrant family. They had traveled from their home in central Europe to farm the rocky soil of northern Minnesota. By hand they dug rocks from the fields, built stone walls, and planted corn and rutabaga. They raised chickens and milked several cows. Grace shouldered major responsibility for the younger children. She bathed, dressed, and fed them. Space was limited and children slept together for warmth. An invalid grandmother lay on the couch closest to the stove; as she became feebler Grace assisted her mother by heating her bath water and sponging her wrinkled skin. The mother's chief concern was not to prevent the children from viewing the grandmother naked, but to keep the grandmother covered from the cold. Children often watched each other's bare bodies and in the summer would skinny-dip together at the river.

An unlocked privy supplemented by a pot in the winter was the family bathroom. Grace remembered that the younger children, and sometimes the older, would creep behind the privy and peer from beneath to catch another while enthroned. She remembered a game she played with the infant boys. She tickled the penis to make it grow "like a flower," while the other children pointed and giggled. One little brother asked the parents at the dinner table about a thumping noise he had heard the night before. The father smiled at the mother and said, "We were making babies; you've got to make a lot of noise to make healthy babies." The other children grinned and glanced at one another. Later they provided their less sophisticated sibling with a detailed and fairly accurate description of what had occurred the night before. Another time Grace's four-year-old sister was absent-mindedly rubbing her crotch on the bedpost. The father covered her with a blanket, claiming that she was distracting the others who were supposed to be studying.

Partly because the farm was isolated and partly because of family custom, Grace was not courted until she was almost nineteen years old. Six months later she married that same young man, also from an immigrant family. Although both were naïve and clumsy, Grace experienced regular orgasms after the first few months of marriage.

Despite diverse religious, educational, and cultural backgrounds, these families reared children with healthy attitudes about sex. What did they have in common? First, the parents were comfortable with their own sexuality, and freely communicated this to the children. Second, they maintained a balanced perspective, according sex a position among other important values. They didn't overemphasize eroticism through shame or punishment, or underemphasize it through avoidance. Achievement was not allowed to overwhelm pleasure, and pleasure did not supersede consideration for others. Third, parents approached eroticism just as they approached other important developmental aspects. The family actively shaped and channeled the direction and expression of the sex drive. Fourth, the children's independence was encouraged so that sexual interests would extend outside the family; the guilt and frustration which would otherwise result were thus avoided. Fifth, parents provided an experience in intimacy, which imbued sexuality with depth and substance. With humor and tenderness these parents enriched and strengthened their children's sexuality.

4

DIRTY OLD MEN

THE RECENT LIBERALIZATION OF SEXUAL ATTITUDES DIDN'T
spring full-blown from the "in" generation. It arose from the
toil of researchers and writers for over a century. Edward
Brecher, in his book *The Sex Researcher*, has traced changes
in attitudes about sex through the growth of the sex researchers themselves. The first of these, Krafft-Ebing (1840–
1902), made an honest attempt to catalog and describe sexual
aberrations. He mobilized his readers' terror and disgust by
detailing the most horrifying cases of sadism in the history of
criminal law and did much to further the rigid repression
in the latter half of the nineteenth century. *Psychopathia
Sexualis* stressed that the simplest acts between lovers were
perilously close to perversion. An innocent kiss served as the
precursor of a monstrous act. Perversions were the inevitable
sequel to childhood masturbation. Guarding the child against
self-abuse saved him from the insane asylum or the gallows,
and protected future generations. Krafft-Ebing described one
woman who began to masturbate as a child and continued in
marriage even during her twelve pregnancies. Due to this,
five of her children "died early, four were hydrocephalic and
two of the boys began to masturbate." The fate of the twelfth
child was not recorded.

It remained for Havelock Ellis and his contemporary,

Sigmund Freud, to alter the cultural climate. Havelock Ellis was born in 1859 and died in 1939. His childhood was overwhelmingly Victorian. None of his four sisters ever married and Havelock himself remained a virgin until his marriage at thirty-two. He was exposed to all the antierotic horror stories with which Victorians stuffed the minds of their children at an impressionable age. Although his books never gained the preeminence and worldwide popularity of Krafft-Ebing's melodramatic work, he was the first to proclaim that masturbation is normal and perhaps a necessary part of healthy development in both boys and girls. He presented human sexuality in an altogether different context, as a pathway to joy and fulfillment. Several years in advance of Sigmund Freud he published a series of case histories which delineated the vast range of sexual experiences and interests among young children. He included not only those who were later identified as perverted or criminal, but also children who grew up to be happy and healthy pillars of society. He indicated that the early repression of sexuality in girls was a major factor in female frigidity. He anticipated Kinsey and Masters by describing male impotence and female frigidity as psychological in the overwhelming majority of cases.

His motivation to become a physician and to collect and publish his gargantuan eight volumes, *Studies in the Psychology of Sex,* stemmed from his own sexual problems. Instead of rationalizing or denying his partial impotence, he developed openness, which enabled him to accept homosexuality without prejudice, and to rework his own sexual conflicts. At the age of sixty, Havelock Ellis finally found full sexual potency with a young French woman who loved him. They lived together happily until his death at the age of eighty. He was the first to dispel the stereotypes of his time, emerging as the true father of the "sexual revolution."

Sigmund Freud also developed within the Victorian corset. Normal sexuality had been defined as the occasional insertion of a husband's penis within his wife's vagina in order to procreate—never recreate. Even Freud taught that masturbation sapped strength and produced a debilitating disease: "neurasthenia." He echoed Tissot, who had proclaimed a century before that the loss of one ounce of semen sapped as much strength as forty ounces of blood. Yet Freud was a liberal. He refused to resort to the accepted treatments for self-abuse, such as the application of a white-hot iron to the clitoris. Instead, he recommended persuasion and surveillance around the clock. He identified sexual deviants such as the exhibitionist and Peeping Tom as childlike rather than the carriers of a loathsome disease. He removed sexuality from the Calvinists' bailiwick of evil and stated simply that sex is a natural and necessary developmental force. He emphasized that children perceive eroticism differently from adults.

Freud provoked immediate furor in 1903 when he presented his treatise on infantile sexuality. The concepts that infants are erotic and that normal sexual development is essential for health shocked and angered Victorian Vienna. Freud was ridiculed and his theory soundly rejected.

Freud describes the child's sexual development in narrowly defined stages: oral, anal, genital, and latency. Although these concepts are laced with profound insight, they are also somewhat misleading. He assigned the mouth as the sexual organ of infancy and the anus as the sexual organ of the toddler. Genital sensations don't arise until about the fourth year, only to be submerged in "latency" a few years later. Genital pleasures are not experienced again until puberty. (Freud, 1953) We know now that any area of the body can become an erotic focus at any time. In "latency" there is a steady increase in sexual interest and activity. In spite of these discrepancies, Freud stands correct in his basic assumption: Sex begins in infancy.

Freud elucidates a number of defenses, techniques we use to avoid anxiety. An idea may be accepted intellectually while it remains rejected emotionally. We know that death is inevitable, but cannot really accept our own demise. We may say that sex is a healthy, normal function and yet feel uneasy with a child's erotic experiments. A mother who certainly wishes her little girl to become a sexually competent adult is "worried sick" when she discovers her five-year-old daughter poking at the family pooch to "make his wienie come out."

Freud was reared in the philosophy of "Kinder, Küche, und Kirche." After dinner, women were excluded as men retired together to the library for brandy, cigars, and good conversation. Freud proclaimed that "anatomy is destiny," and intimated that the clitoris was but a damaged penis. They were expected to stand in awe and envy as they viewed the magnificent male. Sexually inadequate, passive, and socially inferior, women possessed "the charm of a child." Irrational, emotional, and dependent, they could compensate in part by bagging a husband and bearing his child. Men, of course, were aggressive, analytical, independent, and confident. (Gould, 1975)

Today many women still feel inferior to men both in business and in bed. They accept lesser sexual pleasure much as they accept a lesser salary and more menial labor. Tasks such as changing smelly diapers or scrubbing floors remain "woman's work." But women, too, need to feel potent in order to seek, ask for, and occasionally insist on what they need in business or in bed. (Fischer, 1973) Building a sense of self-worth in sexually dysfunctional women is a goal at the sex clinic; building a sense of potency in young girls is a task for the parent.

At the age of sixty-nine, Freud finally accepted masturbation as not debilitating. Perhaps women seemed not quite as debilitated as they did during his youth. In his time Freud was both a prisoner and a revolutionary; Freud changed his culture, and the culture changed Freud.

Now clergymen receive training in sex counseling and there are sex therapists or clinics in every major city. Popular magazines carry material that would have been considered pornographic in Freud's era. Nude beaches and clinging T-shirts with sayings about oral sex are here. We teach sex in the grammar school and allow adolescents into drive-in theaters where the PG-rated show would have been rated triple-X just two decades ago. We wonder whether the male erection will persist in spite of women's liberation. Freud's theories no longer shock us, and yet, three quarters of a century later, we continue to avoid our children's sexuality.

Havelock Ellis faced rejection, Freud provoked ridicule, and in 1948 Alfred Kinsey met renewed furor with the first scientific attempt to define and study human sexuality. He included a study of childhood eroticism because he considered such a study essential to the understanding of the adult response.

He interviewed children as young as age two and found that many had learned about sex around the time they had begun to talk. He noted that girls were much more constricted and inexperienced than boys and related this to the extraordinary incidence of sex problems in women. Those few women who reported childhood masturbation reported a far higher rate of orgasm in marriage.

Kinsey dispelled a tenacious myth which Freud and many others had espoused. "Ladies" were assumed to possess at best an anemic, fragile response; Kinsey unequivocally demonstrated that women have the greater and more durable erotic potential.

In 1966, nearly twenty years after Kinsey began to publish, William Masters and Virginia Johnson demolished another, seemingly impenetrable, barrier. In the scientific laboratory, they observed and recorded approximately 14,000 sex acts and studied the humans who could or could not function. Masters and Johnson came to recognize the immense importance of childhood influences. In *Human Sexual Response*, they state: "Neither this book nor this chapter can be complete without emphasizing an acute awareness of the vital, certainly the primary influence, exerted by early psychosocial factors upon human sexuality, particularly that of orgasmic attainment of the female."

Following Masters and Johnson's revelations, a number of prominent psychiatrists examined and elaborated on their basic postulates. One well-recognized expert is Helen Singer Kaplan, M.D., author of *The New Sex Therapy*. On the basis of her work with countless clients, she describes our society as sexually confused and constricted. She states: "Conflicts between sexual wishes and fears of retaliation from gods, society and parents are ubiquitous and perhaps unavoidable to some extent in our society with our current child-rearing practices . . . every manifestation of a person's craving for sexual pleasure is apt to be denied, ignored or treated as a shameful thing, and in general relentlessly assaulted with painful associations and consequences, especially during the critical childhood years." It is the very intensity of the sex drive that creates its vulnerability. It can be distorted, constricted, dehumanized, and even entirely eliminated by early, severe trauma. "This phenomenon is well known to the horse breeder who carefully pads the breeding stall, lest his expensive stud injure himself during coitus and thus refuse to mate thereafter."

Kaplan and others delineate a series of problems that produce sexual impairments. Fear of failure is a frequent cause. This arises from ignorance, misinformation, and trauma. One or both partners are too ashamed or frightened to ask for what feels good. The couple forgoes stimulating investigations for the safety of a routine as familiar as emptying the trash. Women especially may limit sex to "when he wants it." Passively, they accept whatever they happen to get, assuming that mutual pleasure is unattainable or unimporant. Some fear exposure more than failure. "I'd look stupid if I did that" is a common complaint. Women who feel dumpy hide in flannel nightgowns and fake a climax. Men feign indifference when their erections falter.

Performance anxiety is the bane of the male who is overly concerned with pleasing his partner—he assumes total responsibility for her orgasm. If she fails, so must he. He must become erect immediately, use the right foreplay, and continue thrusting until her climax. Making love is a contest where he must measure up or flunk. A single soft erection becomes a catastrophe.

All these problems are perpetuated by the couple's inability to share their concerns or devise realistic strategies together. Hampered by shame and disappointment, they may find it easier to abandon lovemaking. Some may listlessly follow the same old recipe even though the result remains tasteless. Yet erotic impediments are not "just human nature." The sex clinics clearly indicate that sexual attitudes and behaviors are *learned*. Adult dysfunctions result from having understood the body or its function as bad, shameful, or dirty as a child.

If adult problems stem from faulty learning, then the solution is to relearn healthier perceptions and behaviors, perhaps through a series of remedial exercises. Sex therapy clinics do exactly that. Couples are successfully treated without lengthy psychotherapy by undertaking and discussing simple erotic tasks—simple enough to be called "childish." The most basic assignment consists of nongenital touch, or mutual pleasuring. The couple snuggle, rub, fondle, and lick to recapture the springtime of their pleasure.

The touch, smell, and taste of the partner are vital once more. Spirited tussles and frivolous giggles result. Erections are magically resurrected and tissues are once again moist and glistening, ready for the next exercise. More advanced tasks are more difficult; they provoke anxiety and shame. Each partner must stand naked before a triple mirror and beneath a bright light. Each anatomical feature is touched and described. Each must masturbate before the other. Each must relate his or her most intimate fantasy in lavish detail. Role-playing an orgasm, quiet containment of the penis in the vagina, reading erotic books together, and using slang sex words to increase excitement may be other assignments. As these tasks are successfully completed, the couple builds confidence and is better able to communicate. Erotic enrichment and the relief of anxiety are happy by-products.

Our more fortunate children are astutely completing the same tasks, and many more—beneath the porch, behind the bush, and up in the tree house. Our children can treat themselves, if only we will allow it.

5

SEX DYSFUNCTION
IN CHILDHOOD

THE RECOGNITION OF SEXUAL FUNCTION AS A LEARNED RE-
sponse explodes one of the most damaging concepts of our
century: that sexual problems necessarily connote far-reach-
ing emotional problems or mental illness. Conversely, an excellent sexual performance doesn't mean mental health or
the absence of emotional problems. The presence of good
sexual function merely means that there has been the opportunity to expand and develop the sex drive, in the absence
of specific trauma. Sex therapists enable the dysfunctional
adult to develop expertise and accrue confidence through re-
warding erotic experiences. Therapy simply provides the
opportunities and encouragement which rightfully should
have occurred in childhood.

Parents today are vastly more sophisticated than past generations. They seldom traumatize the child with threats or
punishment. Adult impotence or "frigidity" is rarely based
on paralyzing fears or raw revulsion. Today's common problems arise from misinterpretations, shame, anxiety, and a
lack of self-confidence. Today's concerns are: "What if he
doesn't like my breasts?" "Maybe I smell bad," "It's not as
firm as it should be," "She doesn't enjoy it as much as she
should," and "I'm not hung like that horse she was married

to before." Sex traumas are quite insignificant compared to yesteryear's threats of insanity and clitoral cautery. Now the traumas are subtle, such as being caught with your pants down, an unfavorable comparison with another boy's penis, or a chance bathroom confrontation with a naked parent. Yet these relatively minor events somehow result in sexual problems that bedevil an estimated fifty percent of marriages. Small traumas can produce such profound effects only if the child already feels sexually inadequate, confused, or ashamed. This happens because we parents don't transmit enthusiasm, provide direction, or aid in the development of a firm erotic base.

The following cases illustrate how parents unknowingly contribute to the child's low sexual self-confidence and susceptibilty to minor trauma. Most of these examples are of normal children raised by well-accepted methods.

DAVID

David was the youngest of five boys born to stable, intelligent parents who were both college graduates. Although the parents had moved away from a literal interpretation of the Bible, they attended church regularly and taught their children responsibility, patience, and good work habits. The older boys were successful and productive community members.

David was a "late blessing," the youngest by ten years. He received more attention and had fewer responsibilities than his brothers. When he was three years old he enjoyed rubbing and pulling at his penis while sitting on the toilet. His mother observed this and hastened to zip his pants up. After that she made certain he had a book or toy to occupy his time while enthroned. She was careful not to leave him there too long. About a year later David observed one dog mount another and ran to ask his father what they were doing. The father threw a stick and shouted so that the dogs ran off. By age five David's sex education consisted of his Sunday school teacher's comments on certain Bible stories. He knew that adults were upset if he opened doors without knocking, but the most he had ever witnessed was his mother in bra and panties.

When he was six, his favorite older brother eloped with a girl of a different faith. David missed his brother. He sensed the family turmoil and his father's anger. He overheard his father say that this was "the worst thing that could ever happen." At age seven, David related a joke he had heard at school about a little boy who took a bath with his mother. The same tale that had evoked uproarious laughter from classmates was greeted by stony silence at home. His mother said it was not a nice joke and not to tell any more like that. Shortly before this incident, David had begun playing with his penis again, this time carefully concealed under the bed-covers at night. After the joke fiasco he stopped pleasuring and wondered if dirty thoughts had made him bad, like his favorite brother who had never returned home. Over-whelmed by feelings of guilt and worthlessness, David spent long hours alone and exhibited some puzzling behavior. He neglected his chores and was reprimanded; he forgot to take a pencil to school until his teacher sent home a note. Al-though he had been an excellent student, the letters and syl-lables seemed hopelessly mixed and he began to fail in reading. Every type of remediation was ineffective. David's parents were frustrated, angry, and concerned.

Finally, David was brought for psychiatric treatment. Dur-ing the first months of therapy, he played listlessly and remained aloof. He filled a pail with sand and dumped it again and again. He worried that his hands were soiled, and often visited the bathroom. In the third month, he smiled spontaneously and began to use a variety of playthings—puppets, paints, Play-Doh, and dart guns. Now he enjoyed our sessions "a lot." One day we talked about how babies were born. David was silent and picked at his ear. Suddenly he asked if babies would die from "dirty things." Even with my reassurance he refused to elaborate—instead he struck the long-nosed alligator puppet again and again against the sink. In the next session David was sullen and distrustful. Once more he poured the sand from one vessel to the next. Silently I modeled a large red Play-Doh penis on a baby doll. He stared at it intently for several moments. Abruptly, he flew at the doll and smashed the penis with his fist. "I know what *that* is!" he screamed. In the weeks that followed, more organs were constructed and demolished. I asked if he ever wanted to do that to himself. There followed a torrent of words interspersed with tears. His penis was "dirty, rotten, evil, and it stinks." This was because he had played with himself even though he knew it was bad. He said, "If you did that God would hate you and kick you out of your house."

David's parents were astonished. They had never punished David or told him that sex was evil. Fortunately, they understood, and reassured David that he was not bad and would not be sent away. His father gave him permission to masturbate by relating his own early pleasures and concerns. David again read fluently and remembered to take pencils to class.

Because David had little positive information or experience, he grossly misinterpreted events. Ashamed and miserable, he attempted to deny all erotic feelings, engaging only in clean respectable activities. This was all too much for David, and so he became symptomatic. If David had had reassurance, encouragement, and permission to engage in sex play, therapy would have been unnecessary.

MEG

Meg was the younger of two children born to a couple who seemed absolutely mismated. Meg's father was a complaining, jealous man who rarely said anything nice. Mother was highly erratic. She purchased expensive dresses and worthless baubles, depleting the family bank account. She reacted to her husband's recriminations with profuse tears. If this wouldn't deter him she threatened to leave, once screaming that the only reason she hadn't left years before was because of "those stupid brats." When not upset, she was an adequate but uninspired mother.

Meg recalled her childhood as filled with uncertainty. When she was five, her parents separated and she was sent to live with her grandmother, where she remained for three years. The grandmother was an unwilling sitter who only accepted her charge to "keep her out of the orphan's home." It was then that Meg encountered an exhibitionist in the alley behind her grandmother's apartment. Instead of fleeing, she crouched against the wall and stared wide-eyed at his full erection. He approached and ejaculated within a few feet of her face. She never told anyone, assuming they would be angry. She knew little about sex, although she had participated in a few mild sex games and had seen a film at school.

Intelligent and hardworking, Meg was granted a scholarship to a prestigious university. There she became known for her ability to organize student activities. She maintained her composure under difficult circumstances, once intervening successfully for a classmate who was being expelled. She dated frequently, petted occasionally, but remained a virgin. At age twenty, she realized that she was the only neophyte in her entire circle of friends. Not to be different, she acquiesced on the next date, an event she later referred to as her "backseat initiation ceremony."

Following graduation from college Meg was uneasy. Several of her friends were married, and others had moved away. Her position as a management trainee in a large department store presented little challenge. During the next six months she selected, attracted, bedded, and wedded the son of the owner of her department store's largest competitor. She felt comfortable as a newly married young woman, although she was only vaguely aroused in bed. Having studied Kinsey, she recognized that this was not unusual. She awaited the orgasms which were sure to commence after several months or years of marriage. When she and her compliant husband finally arrived at the sex therapy clinic, she had already visited gynecologists, tried acupuncture and hypnosis, and had even obtained the female equivalent of a circumcision. Repeated failures had increased her sense of inadequacy.

It's tempting to blame Meg's sexual problems on her encounter with the exhibitionist. Indeed she was "traumatized," but in large part because she already felt utterly helpless—unable to flee or become angry. Adults had always seemed threatening and unpredictable. She had never seen a penis under more favorable circumstances or received any positive messages about sex. Greater confidence in any area, but especially sex, would have lessened the impact. As an adult, Meg's gravest fear was criticism. To prevent this, she strove for perfection by doing all the "right" things. An orgasm became a product like a management report or a well-decorated room. The more anxious she became, the more elusive her pleasure.

HERB

Herb was seven when he was brought for psychiatric evaluation because he had bluntly asked several little girls to lower their panties so he could look. After one distraught mother complained, Herb's father told him that it wasn't right, and not to do it again. Herb seemed to understand, but attempted to pull down another girl's panties that same afternoon.

Herb's early development was unremarkable except for clumsiness that kept him from hitting a baseball and being chosen for a team at school. At the age of four he had been circumcised because of adhesions and infections about the foreskin. Herb had not asked questions nor did he appear anxious before the operation. After the surgery he cried plaintively, but soon was quiet.

In his first session, Herb appeared to be a wide-eyed lad

with a slight stutter and a need to please adults. He wouldn't discuss his voyeuristic activities at all. After several months he asked to see his female therapist's genitals. She had some difficulty in dealing with this request and Herb steadfastly refused to discuss his reasons. Eventually she provided him with pictures, diagrams, and explanations. He next asked her to view his "wee-wee." This she did, reassuring him that it looked perfectly all right. Herb appeared relieved, and for the first time asked her if she had any children of her own.

Prior to his circumcision, Herb had no idea whether his penis was good, bad, or indifferent because no one ever talked about it or paid any attention to it. He thought it might not be too good because it was always covered up. When the infection began he was told not to touch it because it would get dirty. Then the operation removed something and made his penis better. Also, it hurt—so it certainly must have been bad. Herb's voyeuristic penchant was an attempt to gain information and reassurance. Were girls like that because they were dirty and had an operation? Would he have another operation and become a girl? What if he didn't touch his penis so that it would stay clean? Was it clean now? Could adults like his penis and want him to keep it? All these questions would have been unnecessary if Herb had known before the operation that his penis was handsome and valuable in the eyes of his parents.

WARREN

Warren's parents were well-to-do. His father was the owner of a successful chain of restaurants and often traveled about the country. His mother did little in the father's absence, since there were servants in the house, including a governess for the two young boys. The governess kept the children clean and neatly dressed. She took them to the Tiny Tot's Theatre and taught them not to interrupt adult conversation. Although the father had little to do with the children he maintained high expectations for their behavior much as he did for his own.

When Warren, who was the older boy, was reported by his second-grade teacher for stealing a rock specimen, father twisted his ear. Later Warren twisted the ear of the family dog. The next summer Warren persuaded a neighbor girl, a year older, to play "Mommy and Daddy" with him. Although Warren had never spied on his parents he had studied copulating animals and a sex manual from the family library. His game consisted of placing his three-inch-long erect penis between the thighs of his partner. For months following this event he extorted money from the neighbor girl by threatening to tell her parents. At age nine he was routinely stealing money from his mother's purse and by eleven he was depleting the family's liquor supply. The parents presented him for psychiatric evaluation at age thirteen after he informed his father that his mother had taken a lover. Through this falsehood he had almost demolished the parents' marriage. Mother recalled that she had fired several servants that year because of Warren's reports of clandestine activities.

When Warren was seen alone he readily admitted his fabrications and spontaneously recounted a list of ingenious misdeeds. One of the maids who had been fired had refused to grant him sexual favors, although her successor had been coerced into doing so.

Warren's governess had felt it was not her responsibility to tell the boys about sex. Her close supervision of all their activities had effectively prevented any sex play when they were young. By the time Warren was five he had discovered that "dirty words" were a sure way to upset his governess, who would not tell his parents for fear of losing her job. Sexuality became a powerful tool for revenge.

ANN

Ann was the only girl among three children born to a minister and his wife. Both parents were content in their life's work and in their relationship to one another. Ann's mother gave her children more than adequate nurturance in spite of church-related duties and the fact that all three children were born in the space of only four years.

As an adult, Ann recalled her parents' emphasis on the daintiness of little girls. "Sugar and spice, and everything nice . . ." She was expected to smell sweeter and remain cleaner than boys, and never to fight back. Boys could show off and do "dirty things" that were taboo for girls. At home, sex was alluded to but never discussed.

As a little girl, Ann received more attention than the boys, which was most irritating to her older brother, Richard. He took delight in surreptitiously punching her and then denying it. At other times he would push her in the water or kick her for no apparent reason. Never did he cause her any injury severe enough to leave a mark. At first Ann ran in tears to her mother. Richard absolutely denied any misdeed, stating firmly, "She only wants attention." The mother, busy and frustrated, would tell both to be good and play nicely together.

One day, Richard really was kind to Ann. With two friends he inveigled her into an excavation in a nearby wooded lot. They had "something really good" to show her. Once in the pit they proposed a contest to see how far each person could project a stream of urine. The winner would receive a candy bar. Softened by her brother's solicitude, Ann agreed to compete even though she realized that her equipment was not the best. The boys clapped, laughed, and peered closely as Ann made an unparalleled attempt. Ann recalled the experience as a pleasurable one, more for her brother's acceptance than for the erotic sensation. Afterward she felt increasingly guilty and inadequate. Her brother had lost interest in the game and in fact had found a new pastime. He required acts of servitude from Ann such as scratching his back for hours or bringing him food in the middle of the night. She had long since ceased complaining to her parents.

Compliant and well-mannered, Ann was never identified

as a problem in childhood. She remained a virgin until the age of twenty, when she married a conventional young man who taught school. This union produced three children in five years. At age twenty-six Ann entered therapy. She could not identify a specific problem except that she was making her tolerant husband miserable. During the day she followed a rigid, joyless schedule which allowed her no time for herself. At night sexual expression was precluded by twenty rules. Her husband could not expect sex when the children were awake, in the week prior to or during her menstruation, after a heavy meal, while she was pregnant, in the early morning, or in the evening after ten o'clock. Her husband avoided placing any more demands on his already overworked wife.

Tractable, clean, and inhibited, Ann was shaped by her parents' teachings. As she had not been taught that sexual pleasures were nice, she assumed they were part of the aggressive, dirty delights reserved for boys. Too frightened to express her resentment of males directly, she barricaded herself and denied her husband sexual pleasure.

SHIRLEY

Shirley was clearly her father's favorite little girl. She had inherited his red hair, good looks, and "feisty" manner. The father preferred her company on walks and in the car. When the family watched television, Shirley's place was on Daddy's lap in the reclining chair. The mother denied any jealousy but gave Shirley less attention than the others because she had so much from the father.

Shirley did not remember any early sexual information or experiences although she knew that her brothers also enjoyed touching her. At about age eleven she thought her father had an erection while she snuggled against him. Afterwards he was more restrained and no longer allowed her on his lap. Among classmates Shirley was the most popular girl, known for her cheerfulness and vivacity. During high school she fell in and out of love at least ten times. She wished to become an actress or a stewardess, but her grades were quite mediocre.

Following high school Shirley worked briefly at a soda fountain while she dreamed of other careers. At the age of nineteen she met and quickly married an airline pilot and then moved to rural Arizona. There she felt lonely and developed splitting headaches. She anticipated Friday nights when her husband was home and would take her dancing. At the dance hall she flirted with other men and talked incessantly. Shirley was furious when one Friday her husband indicated that he would rather stay quietly at home. She accused him of being inconsiderate and capped her grievances by screaming at the top of her lungs that he had given her no orgasms in the four years they had been married. This came as a surprise, because she had always faked her response. Shirley's husband used this inadvertent disclosure as a wedge to involve her in joint marriage counseling.

Shirley's early life with her indulgent father was like a giveaway show without any need to earn approval. She received every gratification without effort. Her sexual response remained as immature as her character. She married another "Daddy" and expected him to provide infinite attention with little responsibility.

JOE

Joe was the younger of two brothers. His mother was a divorcée who supported the family by working as a supermarket cashier. Joe never knew his natural father, who had disappeared shortly after his birth. When Joe was three years old there was a stepfather in the house for several months. He drank every evening and was often too sick to work. Older brother Cliff cared for Joe while Mother worked. Discipline consisted of a kick or a shove and a threat that worse might happen if Joe ratted on him. In preschool years Joe was timid and remained as close as possible to his mother. When she was gone he played with the little girl next door in spite of Cliff's taunts. When he was six some older boys forced him to rub and lick her genitals. Then they laughed at him and pushed him out of the garage. Terribly ashamed, he never told his mother. In the second grade he was bullied, bruised, and heckled as a "baby." Finally, Mother and Cliff decided that Joe must learn to fight back. His grandfather bought him boxing gloves and entered him in a karate school. Joe not only learned to retaliate but developed a reputation as a small but scrappy kid.

At age twelve Joe was given a dirt bike. With an ear-splitting roar, he soared over ditches and raced with his friends around the dump. Throughout high school he preferred tinkering with his motorcycle to studying or going out with girls. By the time Joe graduated, most of his buddies had sweethearts who rode behind and watched the races. Gradually Joe began to like Mary, his best friend's sister. Mary described Joe as quiet but deep. She liked to talk and felt that Joe truly understood her. After several months they were married.

A year after the wedding Joe was employed as a mechanic and still spent his weekends riding motorcycles in local races. He didn't drink or gamble, and he brought his paycheck home regularly. He expected his meals to be ready on time and the house to be clean. Mary was pregnant with their first child. She wished she had trained as a practical nurse before marriage. She described Joe as insensitive and less interested in her than in motorcycles. Lovemaking was perfunctory, and Mary was left irritable and restless. One evening she began to suck on a cough drop at bedtime. Joe's sketchy foreplay, penetration, and rapid ejaculation happened so fast that the cough drop was still intact when he finished. When Mary attempted to discuss this with Joe and a marriage counselor Joe looked uncomfortable and changed the subject.

Joe's mother was distinctly disenchanted with men and sex. Joe sensed this when he was small and had scant opportunity as he grew to become comfortable with sex or the male role. His first erotic contact with the little neighbor was an insult superimposed upon countless humiliations. With time he salvaged his self-esteem by becoming a daredevil on a motorcycle. After marriage he remained closer to his cycle than to his wife. While observing the superficial requirements of marriage, he avoided any emotional investment. He derived major gratification astride his leaping, smoking Yamaha. No one would ever call him a baby again.

KAREN

Karen was the only child born to a strikingly beautiful woman. Her parents lived in an expensive suburb where Karen attended a private school. Her mother disliked suburbia and had few friends; yet she made no plans to live elsewhere. At times she was resentful and jealous of her often absent husband. The mother devoted hours each day to Karen, who was her confidante. The mother's beautician did Karen's hair each week. The mother relied on Karen's good humor and vivacity to buoy her sagging spirits.

When Karen entered school she chose her girlfriends and organized a "Candyland Club" for the select few. Karen suggested a game called "Reform School" in which she somehow was always the teacher. She preached, gave assignments, and pretended to spank "bad" children. She instructed some to pull down their panties, and others to disrobe completely, so that she could "inspect." She rewarded this "good" behavior with candy treats, which were in constant supply. Karen herself never disrobed.

At age ten Karen was given a lacy nightgown and a catered birthday party by her mother. Her father was away on a business trip. Karen began to date at age thirteen, and on her return, promptly reported all happenings to her mother. They giggled and whispered far into the night. Her mother was certain that she could trust Karen because they were so close.

Karen became pregnant in her junior year of high school. She told her mother immediately, but both concealed the fact from her father until Karen was in her sixth month. Her father was enraged and blamed the mother. The mother indigantly accused him of long-term neglect and indifference. For the first time in years both parents acted together when they brought Karen for psychiatric evaluation. During my session alone with Karen she confided that she had not even liked the father of her child, that sexual relations were mildly disagreeable, and that marriage was a real "turnoff."

Karen received copious erotic stimulation from her mother. This highly charged, intimate relationship restricted Karen and impeded her normal sexual development. The boyfriends and the pregnancy served only to provide the mother with exciting material. No male was really important.

Any of these parents could have lived in your community or on your block. Concerned and responsible, they provided all the common necessities. They were functioning members of the middle class who wished their children to become happy, healthy adults. The occasional marital discord or emotional problems were not unusual or incapaciting.

These parents never threatened or punished their children's early erotic explorations. They skirted the area tactfully to avoid trauma, utilizing avoidance, distraction, and vague generalizations. Even the two parents who intensely stimulated their children did little to direct their sexual growth. Children were left to define their own sexuality, through various scraps of information augmented by fantasy. Parental lack of enthusiasm, embarrassment, and reluctance to impart information suggested that sex was different and perhaps shameful. Erroneous conclusions and gross misinterpretations were the rule. Not one parent welcomed a child's early erotic gropings as the hallmark of healthy development.

There were no words of encouragement and no considered guidance.

Several families were deficient in more than one area. Meg's, Warren's, and Joe's families failed to provide an experience in intimacy, and these children suffered severe impairments. Shirley and Karen were stimulated but bound in an exclusive relationship with one parent, which limited both sexual and emotional growth. David, Herb, and Ann were reared with intimacy and encouraged toward independence. They became healthy individuals with sexual problems.

Meg and Joe experienced sexual trauma outside the home which may have intensified their difficulties. Both were acutely vulnerable because of feelings of helplessness and inadequacy before the trauma occurred. They had no basis in erotic competence or knowledge with which to interpret the events correctly. Each had already assumed from their parents' attitudes that genitals were somehow bad or dirty. Neither had had any experience which indicated that genitals could be nice and feel good. Thus there was no protective cushion to soften the emotional impact of horror and revulsion which constituted the trauma. Had these children been better equipped, the "trauma" would have shriveled to a strange or unpleasant "incident."

By not permitting or promoting healthy eroticism, we leave our children bare and blind, without protection, in a world where sex may also be used to hurt.

6

OTHER COUNTRIES,
OTHER STYLES

> It is good for man not to touch woman, yet for fear
> of fornication, let each man have his own wife and
> let each woman have her own husband. . . . But
> I say to the unmarried and to widows, it is good
> for them if they remain even as I. But if they do
> not have self-control, let them marry, for it is better
> to marry than to burn.
>
> —PAUL, I Corinthians 7

AUSTERE AND FRIGHTENING, THE CONCEPT OF SEX AS A NECES-
sary evil and abstinence as Christ-like remains basic to Christianity and to our culture. Intercourse is publicly endorsed
only in the marital bed, where it can be justified by the need
to procreate. Our crotchety Christian conscience condemns
behavior that deviates from this ideal. Among two hundred
fifty cultures surveyed, ours is one of the three most restric-
tive. (Murdock, 1960) Ritual abandonment, premarital freedom, and postmarital options are not uncommon in the rest
of the world. One North American tribe is even said to copulate with porcupines, "by a special technique."

What happens to children when they are allowed sexual
freedom? In some Oceanian and African societies, toddlers

explore each other's bodies, sometimes begin intercourse by age four, and are soothed by rubbing the genitals. Children never need to be told about sex, as they have ample opportunity to observe adults. Sexual growth is a smooth continuum depending for the most part on size, aggressiveness, and glandular function. Liberal cultures, such as Polynesian Mangaia, lend perspective to our own child-rearing techniques. In Mangaia, virtually one hundred percent of women achieve orgasm. In stark contrast, on the small Irish island of Inis Beag, the female climax is unknown or thought to be abnormal.

INIS BEAG

Inis Beag is a small Irish island investigated by John C. Messenger. It is the most erotically barren community ever described by anthropologists. There, three hundred and fifty people relatively isolated from the mainland have maintained a stable agrarian culture for two hundred years. The standard of living is low, the birthrate high, and the family of prime importance. There is neither electricity nor running water, and transportation is via several ass-drawn carts. Agricultural tools are rudimentary and barter remains common. There is little distinction between the life style of the wealthiest and the poorest of the islanders.

Although certain Druidic religious beliefs persist, the people are devout Catholics. The average family has seven offspring. Many mainlanders see the Catholicism of Inis Beag as an ideal not attained elsewhere. The islanders combine an overwhelming preoccupation about sin with an obsessive drive toward salvation in the world to come. Women remain at home except for church-associated activities or an occasional visit to a relative. Men attend parties and dances, play cards, and congregate at the pubs. Late marriage and celibacy are as common in Inis Beag as on the mainland. Sex is never discussed in the home and islanders are monumentally naïve and inexperienced. Boys learn some facts by talking to other boys and watching animals, but girls may not even have done that. Girls understand that they must not look directly at a male or allow themselves to be touched. Premarital sex is unknown, courtship almost nonexistent, and marriages are arranged with little concern for the feelings of the young people involved. The marital bond is primarily of economic and childbearing importance and love between partners is extremely rare. Most people are completely unprepared for the wedding night. Women endure intercourse because to refuse is a mortal sin. The husband initiates sex only in the "missionary" position. Foreplay is crude and clumsy. He quickly climaxes and falls asleep. Men believe that the loss of semen weakens and debilitates. They are unaware of, doubt the existence of, or see as deviant, the female orgasm. Messenger describes one middle-aged bachelor, a man about town who often made love to willing tourists. He is astounded when a girl responds to his fondling with a violent bodily reaction. Although he is aware that some women enjoy kissing and caressing, he can't comprehend a woman's climax.

Nudity is abhorred and there is great secrecy about urination and defecation. Even the dog caught licking its genitals inside the home is whipped and banished from the house. Chickens who defecate while setting on the nest are soon killed and eaten. Underclothes are not removed for sleep or for the sex act. Only infants are completely bathed each Saturday night. Children and adults wash from the neck upward, and the elbow and knee downward. To be caught barefooted is cause for shame, and clothing is always changed in private. Men who brave the ocean in canoes must rationalize their inability to swim. In fact they dare not bare their bodies enough to learn.

Breast-feeding is uncommon because of its sexual connotation. By late infancy, affection is demonstrated by word rather than touch. Masturbation, sex play, and "dirty" words are severely punished. From early childhood boys and girls are rigidly separated in both work and play. Even the fact of pregnancy embarrasses. Pregnancy is never discussed when children are present. Women are considered dangerous during menstruation and for months after childbirth. Children soon perceive that the "good" woman does not like sex.

Malicious gossip is rife in Inis Beag. The fear of rumor is so overwhelming that any hint of sexual desire is carefully avoided. Spying is common, promoting general distrust. A cherished memory once revealed may result in deep humiliation.

Inis Beag is the perfection of Christian morality. All eroticism is systematically constricted from an early age. Not only is premarital sex unknown and adultery rare, but the marital unit is extremely stable. The cost is great.

A commonly held myth is that sexual freedom for children and adolescents will create eventual adultery and thus destroy the integrity of the family. In fact, early license is not necessarily related to marital infidelity. The Andamanese allow their children erotic license, frequently including trial marriages. Yet they practice strict monogamy, both prohibiting and punishing adultery. (Radcliffe-Brown, 1948) The Ute Indians of Colorado and the Tahitians endorse childhood sexuality also, but expect fidelity after marriage. (Opler, 1940) Conversely, a great many cultures which value premarital virginity arrange married life with great license. (Benedict, 1955) In our country, Kinsey reports that "females who had had premarital coitus seemed to have been no more promiscuous in their extra-marital relationships than the females who had had no premarital coitus." While sexual freedom for children will not guarantee, or even foster, fidelity in marriage, neither can we conclude that children's sexual activity will cause infidelity after marriage.

MANGAIA

The rich, tropical islands of the South Pacific contain several sexually permissive cultures, such as Samoa, studied by Margaret Mead, and that of Polynesian Mangaia, studied by

Donald Marshall. Dr. Marshall provides us with a wealth of detailed material on this southernmost Cook Island. His data are supplemented by my own observations in Mangaia and neighboring Rarotonga.

Mangaia is located 650 miles southwest of Tahiti. Five miles wide, it is inhabited by approximately two thousand Maori. The name *Mangaia* means "peace." The economy depends upon the cultivation of pineapple and taro. Villages are tiny, electricity absent, and communication dependent upon one radio transmitter and one weekly freighter from Rarotonga. Mangaians, like other Polynesians, are friendly and open.

Mangaia is an island of lush vegetation, scant income, and many children. Infants are special people, rocked and indulged by all family members. Bare genitals are playfully or casually stimulated and lingual manipulation of the tiny penis is common. Girls' genitals are covered at age four or five, but boys may remain bare until puberty. Privacy is unknown, as each hut contains five to sixteen family members of all ages. Adolescent daughters often receive lovers at night and parents "bump together" so that young children may be awakened by the slapping sound of moist genitals. Although adults rarely talk to children about sex, erotic wit and innuendos are common.

At the age of three or four, children band together and explore the mysteries of the dense tropical bush. Adults encourage this as there are no poisonous snakes or other perils on the island. Fruits grow wild and water is plentiful. Sex play flourishes in the undergrowth and coital activity may begin at any time. Although adults ostensibly discourage sexual activity, its existence is widely recognized and accepted.

Children learn about sex first from one another. Even in 1977, there is no sex education in Mangaian schools. Young girls also learn from elderly women who teach by telling stories and by direct practical instruction. The young boy is taught at puberty by older males. The instruction revolves about the rite of superincision (similar to our circumcision). As the operation is painful, and performed without anesthetic, the boy may delay as long as possible. If he waits too long he may be jeered by girls or accused of having a "stinking penis." He may be knocked out by his friends and then operated on. After the superincision the youth is coached in techniques such as the kissing and sucking of breasts. He is told about lubrication and trained in methods of bringing his partner to climax several times prior to his own ejaculation. Two weeks later, when the wound is healed, a "practical exercise" is prescribed. An experienced older woman acts as mistress and tutor, fortuitously removing the scab.

Before age twenty, boys have copulated with ten or more girls, and at age eighteen they average three orgasms a night, seven nights a week. Girls feel an increase in erotic appetite about the time of their first menses, and soon become orgasmic. Contacts are arranged by the fluttering of an eyelid, or the touch of a hand. Sexual pleasure is a chief concern of both boys and girls.

Adolescence is the "golden age" of erotic pleasure without responsibility. Parents recognize and silently condone their children's vitality. As pregnancy is thought to result from making love with the same man too often, there are frequent changes of partner with a tremendous increase in sexual knowledge and awareness. In fact, girls usually do not conceive until early adulthood. Pregnancy itself often inspires the couple to marry, unless either set of parents strenuously objects. With pregnancy, marriage, and other adult responsibilities, the "golden age" of sexual freedom ends.

Divorce is rare in Mangaia, and its rarity is perhaps related to the years of trial and error which precede the wedding. Infidelity after marriage is uncommon, with two exceptions. First, the wife may always return to the man who introduced her to sexual pleasure. This custom is recognized (if not appreciated) by the husband. Second, a prolonged separation is expected to result in unfaithfulness, especially on the part of the husband. This is ascribed to the irresistible pressures of sex drive. Yet when a husband or wife returns after a long journey, neighbors say they will have to "tie a rope around the house to keep it from being shaken down." Homosexuality, group sex, orgies, fetishism, bestiality, and the use of sex devices are unknown.

Poetic terms describe the character and charm of the genitals. In Mangaia, the penis is beautiful. The clitoris is variously pictured as sharp, blunt, projecting, erect, or protruding. The woman with large hips is like a "bed with a mattress." Undulating thighs rapidly arouse the Mangaian male who relishes plenty of pelvic action. He dislikes sex with the relatively inert European woman. When told that some foreign women cannot climax, he asks, "Will it injure their health?"

They believe that coitus doesn't weaken or debilitate, but that it is a sign of intrinsic strength. If the girl becomes thin, it must be due to frequent sex. Her slimness, which doesn't connote any loss of strength, becomes a public testimonial to her mate's virility. It is an insult to tell a man that he is letting his penis go to waste and "get rusty." The girl anticipates two or three orgasms to his one, via his protracted thrusting. She may achieve a "knockout," an orgasm which lasts up to an hour. She expects foreplay to be brief but skillful. If her partner prolongs foreplay, she may push him away and call him "limp penis." If he doesn't promptly initiate intercourse when they first meet, she assumes she is undesirable or that he doesn't like her. Intimacy may evolve from intercourse, but it is never a prerequisite.

Amid this erotic Eden, there exists one sizable sex dysfunction: impotence. This most likely results from the heavy burden placed on the male. He must copulate without respite or his partner will feel slighted. To conquer her, he must provide her with several orgasms to his one. His climax must be perfectly synchronized. If his partner looks at other men, his virility is questioned. Potent males who have had sex with up to seventy girls are cultural heroes. They have "won the race" and may have a phallus tattooed on their thigh or a vagina on their penis. There are no passive pleasures for the male and each contact becomes a contest. To be average in such a society is a catastrophe. A sword for some and a magic wand for others, the penis remains a captivating symbol throughout all cultures. The erect but fragile phallus is man's greatest pride and gravest peril.

Throughout all fifteen Cook Islands, Mangaians are judged the most independent and the hardest workers. In spite of nightly frolics in the bush, men toil throughout the day in the pineapple fields. Teachers don't assign children homework, as they too labor past dusk. Pleasuring in no way sabotages productivity.

In Mangaia, children routinely witness adult nudity and parental intercourse. In our society, these experiences constitute "traumas," which contribute to neuroses. Here, nudity is discouraged as overstimulating and guilt-producing. Parental intercourse is misinterpreted as "Daddy is beating Mommy." Children react with anxiety and anger. In 1976, liberal Ann Landers writes, "Nudity among brothers and sisters should not be allowed after five years of age. Coeducational bathing should be stopped also." Yet in Mangaia, in the farm commune and in the cramped quarters of the less privileged, these observations are routine and don't result in emotional problems. In Mangaia, children have the advantage of repeated, diverse observations. They soon learn that intercourse is not mortal combat but an enjoyable, mutual transaction. Children adopt a matter-of-fact attitude and begin to note details for future reference. A school principal in Mangaia tells of leaving his sow in the care of a five-year-old neighbor boy for a week. When he returned he found that his sow had come in heat. The child had recognized this and, as a matter of course, bred the sow to a boar some blocks away.

Comfort in seeing, touching, and smelling the naked body

is one prerequisite for a total erotic response. In Mangaia children never have the opportunity to be uncomfortable. The result is an unqualified acceptance of all bodies as innately good. Children and adults are more receptive and less critical. Women who become obese, and most do, are no less attractive, and continue to obtain partners without difficulty. Delight in this easy acceptance is expressed by one middle-aged, rotund Czechoslovakian lady who wears sundresses to town in Rarotonga. She remarks that this would have elicited criticism in any of the many other places she has lived.

In our country most children are reared by continuously clothed adults who always close the bathroom door. Raw flesh, like raw sex, is dangerous—very young children may run about the house nude simply because they are seen as asexual and not too smart at that. As soon as they become more perceptive, prohibitions emerge, flies are zipped, and panties hiked up in public. To wear too little, or the wrong attire, provokes shame and the fear of ridicule. Yet these same individuals are expected as adults to disrobe spontaneously and joyfully relish their naked partner. Alexander Rogawski comments, "Some women inhibited by strict upbringing may have a first opportunity to feel comfortable in the presence of a naked male body when they bathe their own children. This may be followed by greater comfort with their husbands, by more open exchange, and by increased ease with sexual experiences. . . . Parental nudity in itself is not harmful or seductive to children where it is commonplace and part of the culture." Our contradictory attitudes about nudity are but one example of our unreasonable expectations toward sex. Irrationally, we expect the "nice," fully inhibited child to turn over a new leaf and become a sensual, sexually competent adult. Ruth Benedict writes, "The adult in our culture has often failed to unlearn the wickedness or the dangerousness of sex, a lesson which was impressed upon him strongly in formative years. . . . Such discontinuity involves a presumption of strain."

There are only two possible ways to change these inherent contradictions and reduce the strain. One is for grownups to minimize and constrict eroticism, becoming more like the adults in Inis Beag. The other, of course, is to promote the sexual development of children.

The Irish of Inis Beag eliminate the woman's climax and drain the joy from sex. It is a land of corsets and concealment. The master chefs of Mangaia concoct a gourmet feast seasoned with orgasms. Both societies shape the child's erotic response from early infancy. So do we.

7

ENFANT TERRIBLE

A NUMBER OF YEARS AGO THE CHILDREN WHO PRESENTED THEM-
selves to the child psychiatrist were anxious, striving, depressed, or neurotic. They were enjoyable to treat because
they usually got better. The children who lied, stole, or refused to work were handled routinely—by priests, a switch at
school, or parents who were not loath to make their feelings
an important influence in the life of the child. Those parents
sometimes felt helpless and guilty, too, but somehow the child
shared in their culpability so that they were miserable together.

We still see neurotic children, albeit in lesser numbers. But
there are different children in the waiting room now, stomp-
ing Play-Doh in the rug. These are the "enfants terribles."
They are crafty and well aware of their parents' weaknesses
and their therapist's limitations. Reared with copious love and
minimal responsibility, they expect everything and are furious when denied anything. Parental ulcers, high blood pressure, and depression are met with disdain. These self-indulgent autocrats control the family and insist on being the
center of attention. Well-stuffed, protected, and regularly
immunized, they claim eternal nurturance. Life is an umbilical cord attached to an endless reservoir of vanilla pudding. When faced with adversity they push, plead, whine, and
screech; or they tearfully complain, "You never told me."

Undisciplined, with scant social skills, they are disliked by peers and neighbors. When angered they attack a smaller sibling, twist the cat's tail, or accuse their mother of lack of love.

Seen as immature in kindergarten, they are labeled "hyperactive" in second grade and are eventually referred to the psychiatrist simply because the teacher can't stand them. Unfortunately, standard therapy techniques make them worse. The permissive approach, which provides a plethora of toys and encourages infantile behavior, is a recapitulation of their lives. The newest approach is the "positively based behavior modification program." Parents avoid noticing horrid behavior and reward the good. This yields excellent results with anxious, guilty children but scarcely touches these young despots. The psychiatrist can only help the parents develop firmness and common sense. Responsibility is best learned in the home.

The parents are an uncomfortable lot, who endure their progeny as if they were a crown of thorns on the cross of parenthood. They try so hard they make a mess of things. They ask me if children may be affected by food additives, hypoglycemia, or separation anxiety. Their offspring are seeds in the desert which, with love, will sprout and flower. I am the expensive gardener who will magically transform the monsters into marigolds. In fact, children, like flowers, can wilt from too much care.

The first of these children I clearly recall was a small sturdy eighteen-month-old name Angel. He had the knack of turning blue by holding his breath. His mother hovered over him and attempted to divert his attention as he pulled over wastebaskets and skillfully emptied drawers. When she placed him on the couch for a nap, he kicked at her face, twisted, screamed, and clawed at her dress. Finally, like a chameleon, he changed from pink to purple. Mother quickly picked him up.

Another "enfant terrible" was a pert self-possessed young

lady of four. She was piloted to my pediatric waiting room by an exhausted father. He soon lost himself in *Field and Stream*, while she systematically demolished books, toys, and less aggressive children. After several such encounters, I removed crayons, scissors, and all breakable objects from the waiting area. On her next visit she circulated aimlessly about looking for any sharp or gooey object. There was none. She spent a few minutes perusing the large lighted tank of tropical fish. She methodically collected every ash tray in the room, dumped them together, and, standing on a table, unloaded her collection on the fish. Father glanced up from his magazine, groaned, and took her to wash her hands. On their return, she glanced about to see if the toys had reappeared, then settled against Daddy, sucking her fist with legs widespread and her free hand massaging beneath her panties.

After infancy the raw, untutored sex drive is no more agreeable to the observer than any other neglected drive. The glutton who devours all within reach is but slightly better off than a joyless, picky eater. Given parental courage and fortitude, the "enfant terrible" is easier to ameliorate than the listless, constricted youngster. By adolescence, both extremes are quite recalcitrant to any treatment.

How do parents tolerate such extraordinary behavior? They feel battered and hopelessly impotent. They are a fountain of love and an endless supply of Band-aids. They assume that children would be pleasant if free of conflicts and pressures. Therefore they eliminate all possible stress and alleviate every anxiety.

HENRY

Henry was the youngest of two children born to a part-time psychology student in a small university town. His recently divorced mother pedaled a bicycle barefoot to my office. She looked as if she hadn't eaten for days. Jason, her outspoken redheaded seven-year-old, was perched behind her on the bicycle. Strapped to her weary body was a large, ungainly lump of flesh. One hand picked at her shirt while the other was plunged decisively in his mouth. Three-and-one-half-year old Henry distrustfully surveyed his environment.

Once seated in my office, the mother presented Jason as my patient. Jason had been resentful of Henry ever since he was weaned at the time of Henry's birth. Now Jason thought he should be allowed to visit his father whenever he wished, regardless of the time of day or his mother's other commitments. If she refused, he walked the three miles by himself, without even announcing his departure. To avoid problems, the mother permitted Jason to remain at his father's. Just as abruptly, Jason walked home.

While the mother talked, Henry remained strapped to her body, forcing her to sit uncomfortably on the edge of the chair. He fussed and poked his fingers in the crevice of her blouse. Apologetically, the mother explained that she had fed him only two hours before. She unbuttoned her blouse in spite of my reassurance that I didn't mind if he cried. With the speed of a snake, he seized the tiny breast and annihilated it with his mouth. Almost immediately, his eyes turned up, and still sucking, he sank into slumber.

The mother talked about Henry as he sucked. He was heavy, awkward to carry, and predictably vociferous. She had developed many strategies to outmaneuver him. She would nurse him to sleep immediately before leaving to buy groceries. Then she wrapped him tightly about her body so he would not have access to her breast. With a full stomach, and rocked by the pedaling of the bicycle, he slept all the way to town. Once in the store he soon awoke, struggling against his bindings. To avoid criticism, she placed Henry in the cart and attempted to distract him with a toy. Undaunted, he stood precariously on the seat of the shopping cart, emitted piercing shrieks, and snatched at his mother's shirt. His screams became muffled grunts as she clasped him to her chest, burying his body in her coat. She fled down the aisles, snatching what groceries she could with one hand.

Once she hid in a mop closet to suckle her master.

Henry didn't play with other children. He didn't dress himself and only showed a superficial interest in toys. Henry was not retarded; in fact he was a tactical genius who quickly overwhelmed the opposition and established control. He was also a highly erotic child who eagerly sought and achieved sensual gratification. But Henry's behavior was living proof that love is not enough. The child in our culture who still nurses at the age of three or four is rarely trained in any respect. These are demanding, powerful, angry, and distressfully large childen. An old medical school joke tells of a mother who was seen suckling a sturdy six-year-old girl in the waiting room of a county pediatric outpatient clinic. The doctor observed this and asked the mother why she was still nursing such a large child. The mother replied, "I can't stop—every time I try she throws rocks at me."

These children are assertive, uninhibited, and erotically responsive, and each of these traits can contribute to later sexual competence. Yet the sexual response is relatively unimportant. These children are selfish in every sphere. Relationships are predicated on how much they can get, with total disregard for the feelings of others. This hedonism is not only objectionable, but it precludes any true reciprocity.

Fortunately, children do respond to sensible limits and even minimal effective guidance. Sexual responsibility can be taught just as are other kinds of responsibility. For instance, the child of four can be expected not to grab food from other plates or to masturbate openly on a cable car. Our expectations change as the child grows. It is appropriate for a four-month-old infant to squall if suddenly denied the breast, but totally inappropriate for three-year-old Henry.

This attention to training mustn't be so early or so one-sided that pleasure itself is damaged. Before training ever begins we need to permit and encourage the child toward a full range of eroticism, even though sex is experienced in an entirely self-indulgent manner. Before the child can begin to direct the sex drive constructively, he must associate it with pleasure, or he will have no motivation to channel it constructively at all. Our prime time for sex without responsibility is in infancy, under age one. Times of relatively low emphasis on responsibility are the preschool years and the early stages of adolescence. These periods allow additional expansion and elaboration of erotic pleasure, even while the child gradually becomes accountable.

With other drives, we routinely encourage pleasure while we teach. For instance, we urge children to savor the aroma of hot turkey and the taste of freshly baked brownies. At the same time we help them to use a fork properly, and to ask for the blessing. We may intentionally lose a game of slapjack to impart the thrill of effective assertion, yet instruct the child not to slap younger children. We impart little enthusiasm about sex, nor do we condone children's natural eagerness. Yet we do lay down a host of "don'ts" and "not nows." Thus we restrict sex without ever having developed its basic enjoyment. How can we expect children to enjoy sex without experiencing it? Once pleasure is firmly rooted, training can begin.

8

SEX IS WORK

Intimacy IS A TERM OFTEN USED BUT SELDOM DEFINED. As nebulous as *spirit* or *benevolence*, it is not dissimilar to another poorly defined concept, *love*. *Intimacy* is derived from the Latin *intimare* meaning "to put into." The mother and infant who are so completely invested in each other that they appear fused are in a state of total body intimacy. Making love connotes various degrees of mind and body intimacy. Adult intimacy is the ability to blend with another's mind or body and "let go" of many adult constraints. This presupposes comfort and trust—that the other person will not misuse or reject us. If we are unable to trust, we create emotional distance and avoid intimacy.

Sex and intimacy are associated from earliest childhood, when the infant is both close to and stimulated by his mother· A relaxed mother who enjoys holding and talking to her baby promotes both. Her infant learns to like being close as he learns to savor erotic sensations. Through the years, intimacy continues to act as a powerful aphrodisiac. Many a man's flagging erection has been resurrected when his partner rubs his back and they plan together for the future. However, sex is distinct from intimacy and each can exist separately. Sex with little intimacy occurs in the casual liaisons of the singles bar, when a housewife placates an angry husband in bed, or when an aging lothario nourishes his self-esteem in the moans of a protégée.

The vibrator will never replace a flesh-and-blood lover, even when the lover has arthritis and poor timing. This is because the quality of life depends on intimacy—and who can be intimate with a vibrator? Sex serves to enrich and expand intimacy. It cushions the rough spots of living together and provides a vehicle for attachment in a society marked by alienation and loneliness. Many couples communicate directly, by touch, smell, and taste, only in bed.

By rights, intimacy should evolve slowly over the years, to reach its full richness in old age. Unfortunately, this is rarely the case. Intimacy is a will-o'-the-wisp that gradually slips away after the honeymoon, to return, it is hoped, after retirement or when the children are gone. In its place are buttons to push, calls to make, and deadlines to meet. Work rather than love becomes the primary goal. On October 28, 1973, *The New York Times* quoted Henry Kissinger as saying, "What counts is to what extent women are a part of life, a central preoccupation. Well, they aren't that at all. To me women are no more than a pastime, a hobby. Nobody devotes too much time to a hobby." Blazing efficiency in an empty world.

This pattern, in which intimacy diminishes during the productive years, is also rooted in childhood. A great many parents provide the infant with the basic experience in intimacy through body contact, warmth, and snuggling, but demand a high level of performance once the child can think and act by himself. They reward the child for tying his shoes, but not for playing in the sandbox. Copious attention is paid to the alphabet and naming colors, with precious little for blowing bubbles in the milk or rolling in the grass. The most acceptable child is the one who is busy learning or making something useful. Eventually, the child may feel vaguely uncomfortable when he stretches out to read a comic book or when he watches a non-educational show on TV. He has lost the reasonable balance between work and play, doing and feeling, active and passive pleasuring. Freud recognized the danger of overemphasis in either direction when he responded to a question about what a healthy man needs to do. He replied, *"Lieben und Arbeiten"* —"to love and to work."

"Love is work" would characterize many families today. The pathetically familiar suburban wife who frantically volunteers for "anything" is an example. She may feel so depleted after the day's station wagon shuttle, malfunctioning appliances, and parent-teacher conferences that she has little taste for a romp in the hay with a husband who does the "really important" things. One such lady interrupted her mate in the middle of lovemaking to inform him that the toaster was broken. (Schwab, 1974) The career mother may be more harassed than her suburban counterpart, who at least can find time alone to masturbate. The overemphasis on work also takes its toll in the man's erotic response. An eminent sociologist, John Cuber, quotes one wife: "He's their top designer, and everybody knows it. Next year he's sure to be vice-president. But when he gets home at night, he is tired. I make sure the girls are asleep or at least in their rooms. Dinner is late, and just for the two of us—after a lot of drinks. We don't have much sex—but I don't expect it under the circumstances."

The work ethic teaches that business must come before pleasure, and utility before beauty. Sex as a duty to one's mate remains high on the priority list, while sex for pleasure slips toward the bottom. Even play becomes work as the golf course is used to make connections and lunches to cement deals. (Kahl, 1957)

Fun with the family may mean a trip with the kids spent racing from line to line at the amusement park, awaiting a few seconds of kaleidoscopic flight punctuated by nausea. Relaxation is the retreat to the anonymous cocoon of the boob tube, or the peach fuzz in the head after the third martini.

The average middle-class male is also the average male

client at the sex therapy clinic. His impotence may be precipitated by the failure to gain a promotion, or his premature ejaculation a symptom of resentment at his mate's increasing distance and lack of interest. Subtly, sex is now a product also. The sex clinic client would like a list of infallible techniques and is fully prepared to work as diligently as possible. He wishes to get an erection in thirty seconds upon sighting a nude female posterior, and expects to memorize the proper combinations of sensate buttons to press in order to elicit a medium, large, or super-economy orgasm. His problems must stem from a slight malalignment of the sprockets, easily mended by a certain screwdriver which never bends. If cursed with a lone screwdriver which not only bends, but kinks and wobbles, how about an implant? The labor of love is more labor than love.

Many well-educated young men and women make a transition from being young, liberated, and zesty to being old, useful and tired. Marriage is likely to have occurred someplace in the process. Still in their twenties, and fresh from training, the graduates enter the business or professional world. With more money and connections than ever before, they command a variety of erotic experiences. Paychecks are invested in Club Méditerranée rather than house payments. Evenings are spent dining by candlelight, and going to concerts and plays. Stealthily, concepts such as stability, security, and responsibility enter. Painstakingly, youth begins to retrace the parents' footsteps. After several years, the metamorphosis is complete, and the young couple looks and acts startlingly like their parents. Filet mignon by candlelight becomes meat loaf at six P.M. so that the children can finish their homework. Leftover sexual sophistication scarcely intrudes upon the air of tired harassment. This marriage is primarily *useful*—it provides an acceptable neighborhood and the most advantageous social contacts. (Cuber, 1974) The children are raised properly, attend the best schools, and take piano lessons.

Socrates reportedly described a similar pattern more than two thousand years ago. The process begins around the time when the child first enters school. He develops a conscience and learns to live by the rules of his parents. Responsibility, punctuality, and production are clearly underwritten as essential. Eroticism and sexual experience are curiously omitted from the list of desirable values. He notes that sex is an uncomfortable or worrisome area for his parents. At best, they seem lukewarm or ambivalent. Yet this is the format which inevitably must become his own, and he has little choice about the matter. These same values persist beneath the turmoil of adolescence and the relative sexual freedom of young adulthood. With very few exceptions, these principles resurface after marriage or a firm commitment. Priority is given to production and punctuality while sex interests lag. This again becomes the erotically impoverished portrait presented to the next generation. Thus the inhibited child grows through a period of sexual freedom which he then must renounce in order to become an inhibited adult who will rear an inhibited child. That this is indeed the case is shown by a study by Wake in which thirty percent of mothers acknowledged that they themselves had had premarital sex. Yet only three percent approved of this behavior for their daughters, and only nine percent for their sons.

There is no question that these upright, moral, industrious parents constitute the backbone of society. They're concerned with the child's emotional well-being and success in life. They support civic projects, higher education, and Little League. They read Spock and attend church. Although they may not laugh at a shady joke in front of the children, they certainly don't blackball sex by threat or punishment. If anything, these parents are too good.

Parents can preserve the child's healthy erotic response without making radical changes in their own behavior. A certain awareness, flexibility, a sense of humor, and the application of accepted principles gleaned from the study of adult sexuality are all that is necessary. The techniques used to expand and elaborate the adult sexual response are every bit as useful for the child, providing the appropriate adjustments for developmental level are made. As parents begin actively to further the child's healthy erotic development, sexual values ascend on the list of priorities. Sex becomes not only acceptable but important, assuming its rightful position as one of a number of essential concerns. There is one danger: Eroticism can be absorbed into the work ethic so that sex becomes an achievement rather than a pleasure to be enjoyed. This can be avoided through provision of time, freedom from distraction, and a balanced emphasis on both active and passive pleasuring.

The psychiatrist in private practice serves primarily the striving, anxious middle class. There is no dearth of case material to illustrate how responsible, hardworking families unintentionally impair the child's erotic response.

MARK

Mark was a junior medical student when he approached me after my lecture. He was neatly dressed in shirt and tie, unlike most University of California students. He needed my help because he was in a slump. He tried to study, but the sentences seemed jumbled. He was unable to sleep and began to drink in order to relax. He spent most of his time in unproductively planning how to study. He developed three different index systems for notes but was unable to read the notes after indexing them. He was so anxious about his studies that he seldom left his room at night. He neglected to write to his mother and sister and forgot to return their telephone calls.

When Mark had first entered medical school, he earned excellent grades and received a special commendation in biochemistry. He elected training in basic science research. He was accepted by one of the best fraternities, which was adjacent to the nurses' dormitory. Although Mark was inexperienced, he soon found several attractive nursing students who were fascinated by his sensitive, sympathetic manner. Intrigued, he spent many an evening chatting and, eventually, in making love. Although he studied less, he ranked in the top ten percent of his class.

Midway through his sophomore year, Mark was introduced to a red-haired, curvaceous nursing instructor several years his senior. She invited him to her apartment for scampi the next night. That evening Mark was vaguely uncomfortable, although the shrimp were delicious and the wine well chosen. After dinner it became clear that the dessert would be served in the bedroom. Mark was impotent for the first time. His partner, who had heard tales of his athletic prowess, was offended and peevish.

By the end of his sophomore year, Mark was less involved with the nurses and more concerned with his school achievement. He felt that the noise of the fraternity house interfered with his studies, so he rented a small studio apartment three blocks from the hospital.

Mark's father was a distinguished professor of economics in a small but well-acclaimed college. He was home more than other fathers, but was largely occupied with lecture notes and the preparation of a textbook. The mother described him as her "absentminded professor." He never remembered birthdays or anniversaries and often forgot to kiss his wife good-bye. Yet he was concerned and thoughtful whenever problems arose. Mark's mother readily shouldered all major family responsibilities, such as paying bills and arranging for home repairs. When Mark reached school age he helped by raking the yard and washing the car.

Intelligent and likable, Mark was elected president of his tenth-grade high school class. He was a part-time printer's assistant for the town newspaper and played an excellent game of tennis. He was shy with girls, although he dated occasionally.

After several months of therapy, Mark associated his poor

concentration and depression to his confrontation with the nursing instructor. Following that, he had systematically chopped away every source of pleasure. He no longer played tennis, listened to classical music, or attended a movie. He drank alone, to quiet his nerves rather than for enjoyment. When his mother asked him about medical school, he replied in vague generalities, although he had always enjoyed her attentions. He felt strangely inadequate, as if he didn't deserve her interest.

One day, Mark recounted a terrifying dream. He was driving along a lovely seacoast on a winding, cliffside road. He jabbered excitedly to his mother, who sat behind him. The road abruptly ended, and the car swerved out of control and plunged over the cliff toward the water. His hands shook as he recalled his terror. Next Mark described a family reunion where he was taken when he was five years old. Because of limited sleeping space he was placed crosswise in a double bed with three girls. In the middle of the night he awoke to find his pajamas warm and moist. He had drenched himself, the bed, and its three other occupants. Mother was mortified. She announced to all that Mark had never in his life done such a thing. Crestfallen, Mark walked by himself at the edge of the creek. Then he remembered a different scene. When he was ten, his family lived next door to a house with many children. Mark persuaded the twelve-year-old neighbor to entice his five-year-old sister, Janie, to give them a "show." The boy agreed although he lacked personal interest, as he saw his little sister nude almost every night. Janie gladly lowered her panties and spread her legs for a candy bar. Mark peered closely but was afraid to touch. Suddenly ashamed, he left the shed, even though Janie wanted to do it again for another candy bar. Thereafter, he avoided Janie and her entire family. He told his mother they were all lazy people. Yet he thought of Janie when he began to masturbate at age twelve. He tabulated each orgasm, timed it, and carefully caught the semen in a tissue.

ELVINA

Elvina was a self-possessed, brilliant college girl who swept into the student health service demanding information. She certainly did not wish to be examined and refused to reveal her concerns to the receptionist. Once in my office, she produced a notebook and fired a list of questions at me. The interrogation was about sex. In high school she had decided to begin coitus in her first year at college and so she did. Unlike many of her classmates, she obtained contraceptive pills through a free clinic. She chose an acceptable young man with similar background. They had sex on the third date. She had not expected to enjoy it the first time and was glad to "have it over with." She continued her sexual activities with other partners but still experienced only mild excitement. She ran the gamut of books, scented oils, marijuana, Kegel exercises, and "poppers" to no avail. She asked me if birth control pills decreased desire, if she could have her glands checked, and if there was an operation which would "rearrange" the clitoris. She definitely did not want therapy.

Elvina described her mother as an ambitious, domineering lady who organized not only her family but sections of the community as well. When Elvina was young her mother's efficiency nearly overwhelmed her. She was terrified of being swept up in the vacuum cleaner by mistake, or popped into the washing machine with a load of soiled clothes. Elvina felt too helpless to complain. She was certain that there was a good reason for everything her mother did. Her mother made sure that Elvina was always suitably occupied. She was to lie down in order to sleep, sit in order to eat or read, and otherwise be up and about some worthwhile task. She remembered no early sex play and doubted if her mother would have allowed such an inefficient use of time. Elvina was a docile but clumsy child who felt especially awkward with friends her own age. In all of her childhood, she recalled only one instance of noncompliance. When she was five years old, her mother served her an inadequately cooked egg. She felt repulsed by the gleaming gelatinous crown with its bloody speck. In spite of her tears, her mother insisted she eat the egg. After the second bite she vomited her entire meal. Thereafter, she meticulously removed any trace of egg white and absolutely refused scrambled eggs. By the time she entered college, she hastily ate the egg white first in order to "save the best part for last."

Both Elvina and Mark were bright, productive students from good, middle-class families. Both perceived the climax as an achievement and dysfunction as a failure. Both were reared in the work ethic without any affirmation of the value of sex. Industry was emphasized to the detriment of passive erotic pleasuring. Elvina worried so much whether she would have an orgasm that sex became a chore. Mark was so devastated by one episode of impotence that he eliminated all gratification. Although Mark was treated through analysis and Elvina entered a sex therapy clinic, both eventually found relief when they learned to relax and receive erotic pleasure without concern for performance. They could have been spared much misery if their parents had prepared them as well for bed as they did for work.

9

SLUM SEX

MY INTERNSHIP AND PEDIATRIC RESIDENCY WAS IN A POOR SEC-
tion of Chicago, noted for its high rate of drug abuse, illegiti-
macy, and violence. Knifings and sexual assaults were nightly
fare in our emergency room. The corpses we pronounced
dead were seldom reported in the daily newspaper. We assumed that if other area hospitals received a like number,
they were just too common to be newsworthy.

In back of our well-lighted, well-policed hospital area was
a ring of condemned buildings, black shells with cracked
walls. Hungry rats and stray dogs poked through the piles
of rubble. Still farther away, there rose a series of stark
angular high-rise apartment buildings. Each was spaced an
equal distance from the other, and each looked exactly like
its neighbor. They were dark gray, constructed of cement
and steel, and designed for low-income families.

The children of the high-rise buildings received care
through our pediatric emergency room. A mother might wait
for six hours to have her feverish infant seen by a harried
resident. A different child was examined every five to ten
minutes until the resident was so exhausted that one face
became indistinguishable from the next. Children were seldom returned for a recheck and we rarely saw an infant who
was well enough to be given his long-overdue routine im-
munizations. Head lice and the crusted sores of impetigo were

common. After several months of this assignment, physicians became callous and worked much as if they were checking parts in an assembly line. Instructions to parents were curt and little opportunity was given for discussion. We were unable to stem the rising tide of human misery.

Our department of pediatrics recognized the dehumanization of this experience. In an effort to reinvest us with charity, they assigned each resident the care of the children in one of the high-rise dwellings. We were to make house calls, vaccinate, recheck ears, and give well-baby follow-up examinations—providing the families permitted.

On the first day of my assignment, I approached my tall gray monolith with misgivings. It was a muggy summer, and wet sheets hung from open windows. No nurse backed me up and no one had requested my services. Placing a few instruments in the pocket of my white coat, I entered the building only to find that the elevator was out of order. Breathless after climbing six flights of stairs, I paused on the landing to find myself scrutinized by five small bright pairs of eyes, none of which were higher than my knee. Here were my patients, partly clothed, alone and untended on the filthy floor. There were no toys and no furniture. A soggy diaper, several empty cans, and old potato chip bags littered the floor.

The children were unresponsive to my overtures. When I asked the oldest boy, about age five, where he lived, he pointed to door number 602. I knocked, and knocked again. Finally, the door opened a crack and quickly closed. As I moved on, it opened again, and my small informant disappeared. The next knock was more productive. I explained my mission to a slight, disheveled girl who toted a tiny infant while a toddler peered from between her legs. She was only seventeen years old. Distrustful at first, she soon admitted me to the apartment and allowed me to attend her children. Eventually I was able to gain entrance to several apartments on each floor. I began to look forward to my house calls. The children giggled as I walked upstairs, and protected their buttocks with their hands. Once the mothers trusted me, they chattered away and solicited all kinds of medical advice.

The apartment building differed from any world I had ever known. The women were pervasively sad, sometimes angry, and often frustrated. Many anticipated no change other than another pregnancy and another birth. Free birth control was available but seldom employed. One young mother dreamed about returning with her three small children to her parents' farm in Connecticut, from which she had run away six years before. She had saved no money and had not written home. She had never informed her parents of the birth of her last infant, who was of mixed racial background.

Sexual matters were often discussed, although sexual pleasures appeared to be rather peripheral. The making and breaking of relationships, the anger at men who didn't seem to care, and hope for one who really would afforded the most conversation and relief from boredom. Little was expected from men and little was received. Coitus was generally brief, with scant foreplay, something to be "put up with." Heavy drinking often preceded the act. Lovemaking was as often associated with rage as with tenderness. One thirty-five-year-old mother slept with a knife under her pillow. When her boyfriend was too intoxicated to perform, she "kneed him in the balls." She preferred aggressive, assaultive men and couldn't tolerate a "fag type." In spite of partners' misuse or indifference, and their own anger or depression, a few women reported an excellent erotic response. Even then, sex had little impact on the bleakness of life.

Each morning, toddlers and preschool children were placed in the barren hallway to play. Toys were not provided because they were stolen or broken, or caused fights. Children soon formed their own social order, based on size and strength. The younger, weaker toddler would huddle silently against the apartment door, thumb in mouth.

These children were well acquainted with sex. They witnessed the advent of new boyfriends and listened at the apartment door. Tiny living quarters and thin walls added to their expertise. Some slept with their mothers even after an "uncle" or a "fiancé" came to stay. Erotic activities in the hallway were an intriguing substitute for toys. Because of apathy or by intent, older children often went without underclothes. Soggy diapers dragged about the knees of others. Children soon learned to stimulate themselves and others. One enterprising four-year-old was observed proficiently penetrating his five-year-old sister. Others wriggled atop one another, groaning and grunting in succinct imitation. Descriptive words were used, most often incorrectly. When I questioned one boy about a term he used while pummeling another, he was puzzled and then happily defined it as "mother's dirty butt."

Once children entered school, they were exposed to the mysteries and the perils of the alley. Boys soon began to join the junior echelon of infamous older boys' gangs. They remained away from home for hours, gaining acceptance through feats of prowess, such as fighting with a rival junior gang member, pilfering from the corner grocery, or grabbing a girl in the garage. Sex play was a pallid term for what existed in the alley. Coitus commenced as early as age four, although ejaculation was generally absent until after age ten. Most young girls returned home directly after school, observing their mothers' admonitions and their own better judgment. A few ran with the boys, buying protection and acceptance in the gang through sex. Far from being valued, they were assigned derogatory nicknames, were callously used as community receptacles for semen, and sometimes beaten or abandoned. The sex act itself was brief, at best a barter, at worst a rape.

There was no question that these children received early and continued erotic stimulation. Yet the boys used sex more for power and proof of masculinity than for pleasure. Status was achieved through daring exploits, strength, and a frequently functioning phallus. The hit-and-run act took less time than recounting the exploit to other males. Sex was often equated with dirt, and the girls so used were debased and disparaged. The cautious girls who remained at home were more respected and were sometimes awkwardly courted.

In the slum sex and anger are companions from earliest childhood. The toddler observes its mother used, abused, and abandoned by her consorts. Occasionally she abuses her mate. The child himself is the recipient of abrupt physical punishment and is abandoned daily in the hallway. Once there, he is subjected to a series of sexual and aggressive assaults, until with growth, he becomes the master of the corridor. The microcosm of the hallway later becomes the macrocosm of the alley.

Boys and girls soon evolve separate roles: the victor and the victim, the one who grabs and the one who withholds, the protector and the protectee, the policeman and the pilferer. Masculine prowess is highly esteemed and heavily reinforced. Little boys who participate in girls' play are ridiculed by both sexes (Rabban, 1950), and beaten by other boys. Dehumanization is the price. The sex act, in itself an aggressive denial of tenderness, becomes the medium of exchange between the two camps. The girl who gives in earns instant ersatz popularity, but lands at the bottom of the social heap. If she resists pressure and withholds, her value increases and she may marry relatively well within the class. (Kerckhoff, 1974) Better to be safe than sorry. Unfortunately, the pattern of withholding and the expectation of abuse is not easy to unlearn. Nor is it simple for the macho male, who for years has "got down on a pig" in the alley, to recapture compassion.

How has this social system affected the sexual response? Kinsey was the first to investigate this in the late 1940's. The lower the socioeconomic class, the more sexually active were the men. In the sixteen-to-twenty-year-old age group with an eighth-grade education or less, the average frequency of coitus was 1.6 times per week for boys, but only 0.3 times per week for girls. In contrast, college men had intercourse on the average of 0.2 times per week, and college women only 0.1 times per week. Thus the difference between classes was much more pronounced for men, reflecting the fact that most lower-class males are serviced by a few promiscuous females. The greater apparent potency and earlier start of the lower-class male was certainly related to the premium placed on aggressive virility and the greater availability of partners.

Lower-class girls were less fortunate. The double standard, dangers associated with capitulation, and lesser overall erotic experience limited their sexual satisfaction far more than the boys'. (Fiasche, 1973) Kinsey found that masturbation to the point of orgasm occurred in sixty-three percent of girls who had gone beyond college but only thirty-four percent of girls who had not gone through high school. Orgasm in marriage followed a similar pattern. The number of women who reached orgasm within any five-year age bracket was distinctly smaller among those with limited education. More of these women never reached orgasm. The lesser the educational level, the less sexually responsive was the woman. A later study by Rainwater of married, working-class couples indicated little expectation for the woman's enjoyment in coitus by either husband or wife. The focus was on male gratification through rapid ejaculation, with scant foreplay or afterplay.

Lower-class women were not as happy either. In 1973, George Gallup reported that only thirty-three percent of individuals with an annual income of three to five thousand dollars saw themselves as "very happy." Happiness escalated with income, as fifty-six percent of those with an income of $15,000 or over were "very happy."

Early erotic stimulation cannot alone protect the sexual

response from distortions and constrictions. The sex drive is colored by the total environment in which it develops. Sex experienced first as an unprotected victim, abandoned in a cold corridor, inevitably becomes associated with fear and rage. To be receptive is to be vulnerable. The child must prove the brutal master or face humiliation. Sex becomes but one weapon in the battle for survival.

10

THE ANGRY ERECTION

SEX AND ANGER MAY BECOME FUSED IN MIDDLE-CLASS HOMES also. The best neighborhoods and the nicest schools have youngsters who use sex as an expression of hostility. The harm is produced not by overstimulation but by specific patterns of parenting.

TIMOTHY

Timothy's mother had always been neat and compliant. She was a high achiever throughout high school and business college. She dressed well and attracted many suitors. She spent hours each night combing and styling her long blond hair. Yet she seldom saw a date more than once and was described by friends as aloof. She never masturbated nor allowed heavy petting, until at age twenty-five she made love with a man she had met at a party that evening. Sex was distinctly unpleasant. Yet such unplanned episodes continued to occur sporadically in the years that followed, always with a different partner. When she discovered at age thirty-two that she was pregnant she didn't consider an abortion. As the months went by she found herself anticipating the birth with pleasure. She decorated the infant's room with taste and all the latest baby-tending appliances. Her competence as a secretary extended to her competence in pregnancy and delivery. She arrived for her prenatal checks on the appointed hour of the appointed day, and delivered easily after only four hours of labor. Although she considered nursing Timothy, this seemed messy and would be inconvenient when she returned to work. Drawing on her savings, she hired a baby nurse for the hours that she was away. She secured the services of the most respected and expensive pediatrician in town.

Timothy was a tractable, engaging infant, entirely devoid of diaper rashes and of odors other than those of the vaguely scented commercial baby products. He was rocked, bathed, titillated, and exhibited in the park.

As Timothy grew, he remained the center of his mother's attention. He learned his alphabet by age four and could recite even lengthy poems from *Alice in Wonderland*. Ensconced in his mother's lap, he was read every Dr. Seuss book in print. Timothy rarely left his mother's side when she was home. Indeed his mother worried that some harm might befall him if he strayed. In the fourth grade he was mercilessly teased by classmates when he walked to school holding his mother's hand. His mother continued to bathe him until he was ten.

During his early years, Timothy was exceedingly happy. His only disappointments were in not being allowed to explore an abandoned freight car or not having permission to join a tree-house club of neighborhood children. Whenever Timothy seemed upset, mother consoled him by a trip to the zoo or a museum tour. After he was ridiculed at public school, mother placed him in a small private academy where he became a favorite of many teachers.

When Timothy was eleven, his mother mentioned to the pediatrician that Timothy had nightmares and still slept in her bed. Following her doctor's instructions, she insisted that he sleep alone. Timothy began to "sleepwalk," stealthily slipping between his mother's sheets at midnight. When Timothy was twelve, his mother woke one morning to find an erection pushed firmly against her satin nightgown. She was alarmed until she realized that Timothy was still sound asleep. She carefully disentangled her nightgown and never mentioned the event to Timothy.

When Timothy was thirteen years old, he began to feel strangely upset. He was restless and it was difficult for him to concentrate. He was terrified by violent nightmares—a car smashed into a building, or a woman was knifed. When younger, he was drawn closer to his mother when frightened. Now he found himself unable to approach her, and too tremulous to sleep. One night, as Timothy tossed restlessly, his mother awoke and attempted to comfort him. Timothy angrily told her to let him be. Confused and hurt, she began to cry. Timothy rose and walked peevishly about the house. Eventually he sat by his mother and consoled her. The next morning, she cooked his favorite breakfast.

When Timothy was fifteen years old, sixteen-year-old Wanda moved into the neighborhood. Her parents were gone almost every night and she soon began to have parties for her friends. Timothy observed her voluptuous dance, heard her laughter, but was afraid to introduce himself. His mother also learned of her liberal young neighbor and was quick to express her disgust.

One Saturday morning, Wanda was mowing the lawn dressed in a bikini. She waved to Timothy and asked him to help her disengage a rock from the mower blade. After that, Timothy talked to her or accepted a soft drink during the hours when his mother was still at work.

During summer vacation, his mother found several issues of *Playboy* magazine carefully hidden between Timothy's mattress and springs. She was torn between a wish to destroy the magazines silently and her concern that Timothy's interest might stem from a lack of proper parental guidance. That evening she delivered a lecture which covered most of the mechanical and moral aspects of sexuality. Timothy stared at the floor throughout the speech. His mother interpreted this as a sign of remorse. When she finished she rose and stood next to him with her arm about his shoulders. She stroked his hair and told him again how much she loved him.

That evening Timothy lay awake listening to the sounds of the party at Wanda's house. Instead of visiting his mother's bed, he dressed and slipped out the back door. He spent several hours sitting on a lawn under a bush, watching the dancing and listening to the music and laughter. When almost everyone had left the party, he entered the house to offer his services in cleaning the mess. Wanda, somewhat tipsy, assumed that this must be a sexual proposition.

Early in the morning, Wanda's parents returned home to an indescribable scene. Not only was their daughter dead, but her vagina was packed with and lacerated by kitchen utensils. Some had perforated the vaginal vault and had entered the abdominal cavity.

The police quickly apprehended Timothy, who was wandering about on the periphery of the crowd. He readily confessed to the crime, although he gave no motive. He denied anger although he admitted that it seemed like an angry thing to do. He saw no reason why he would have used the kitchen utensils in such a bizarre fashion.

This example, however extreme, could be used to illustrate the dangers of sexual overstimulation. Timothy was a very sexy boy. He had been stimulated by his mother for years in ways that could be socially condoned, or at least rationalized. He invaded his mother's bed and certainly savored her physical attentions. Yet Timothy never attempted incest, nor was he lewd or promiscuous. Did overstimulation cause him to rape and kill? And why the savage, senseless mutilation? How did anger come to be linked so closely with pleasure?

Timothy was well taught and well behaved. He renounced other outlets and was a willing captive of his mother's stimulation. At the age of five he realized every boy's oedipal fantasy, for he did indeed possess his mother. In an attempt to please, he restricted himself to the role of good student, engaging child, and mother's helper. As he received considerable gratification for his efforts, he didn't undergo significant conflict until early adolescence. Then he experienced vigorous sexual urgings which, in his setting, were terrifying. His mother aggravated his confusion through her fondling and physical closeness. She teased and stimulated but never satisfied. She noted his erections, but acted as if they were unimportant. Through criticism and moral judgment, she systematically eliminated any other outlets, however innocuous. The invasive quality of her closeness both threatened and disparaged.

Timothy could not express anger at his mother because she was the source of all gifts and goodness. Yet Timothy did feel angry, and his rage mounted as his frustration increased. At last he vented his fury against the second seductive woman in his life. He finally and forceably ruptured the bond with mother. While in custody, Timothy slept by himself.

PETER

Peter was a five-year-old boy presented by his father for evaluation. Peter's parents had been divorced two years before. Now both had remarried. Peter began to spend weekends and vacations with his father, stepmother, and stepmother's young son. During the first visit, Peter did some unusual things. Although well toilet-trained, he stood at the side of the bed and urinated on the carpet. A very concerned father reported to me that Peter's eyes seemed glazed at the time and that Peter could give no reason for urinating. Shortly thereafter, Peter stealthily removed some filmy panties from his stepmother's dresser. He was caught masturbating with them. This pattern persisted in spite of admonitions, counseling, and physical punishment. On the stepmother's advice, the father became increasingly severe, and repeatedly spanked Peter, but the habit persisted. Now Peter made a cache of underwear filched from the laundry pile to assure himself an uninterrupted supply.

Peter later complained to his therapist that no matter how

hard he attempted to conceal this activity, it seemed that he was always apprehended. His habit was far more worrisome than it was pleasurable. His therapist offered him a silver dollar if he could put such thoughts out of his mind for one day. That day Peter pilfered no underwear, but he dreamed about it continuously. Finally he stole another forbidden object, a package of matches, and hid with them behind shrubs in the back yard. His stepmother found Peter lighting a small fire, and he was again whipped. Peter had been imagining his stepmother's panties on fire. Sex for Peter had become a compulsive, angry thing.

FAITH

Faith was the five-year-old subject of a curbside consultation with a pediatric colleague. She was the eldest of three daughters in a stable, strongly religious family. The mother had discovered Faith rubbing her clitoris while bathing. The mother was upset and held Faith's hands under very hot water, saying that she needed to cleanse them from dirty activity. To the parents' surprise, Faith repeated this performance at times and in places where she was certain to be discovered. After spanking her, sending her to her room, and reading her the Bible, they feared she might be diseased and sought the counsel of their pediatrician. This little girl had already transformed a pleasurable act into an expression of anger at her parents. Indeed she had found a weapon which caused them considerable emotional upset and frustration.

The commonest root of the confusion between sex and anger is child abuse. In the slum, harsh punishment, abandonment in the hallway, and persecution by peers converge to make sex a weapon in the battle for existence. But abuse is by no means limited to the slum. In a "good" neighborhood an infant who refuses a heaping teaspoonful of pureed string beans is slapped. A four-year-old who forgets to pick up his toys is called stupid, lazy, and just like his father. A seven-year-old girl is told to fix lunch and then ruthlessly criticized because there are too many sandwiches and she forgot the milk. An eight-year-old boy arriving minutes late for dinner is restricted to his bedroom for a week.

Angry children grow to become angry adults. (Kempe, 1972) The anger can invade any or all areas of expression, but especially eroticism. This is because of the importance of sex, its range and diversity of expression, intrinsic malleability, and above all the fact that the sex drive evolves within the early, intense relationship to the mothering one. Thus the infant who ardently desires his mother's warmth and is left alone in his crib for hours, and the toddler who tugs at his mother's skirt and is roughly pushed away, are seeking erotic, as well as other, pleasures. Instead of pleasure, they receive pain. They feel abandoned and angry. As these youngsters grow they continue to feel deprived and bitter, and they expect the same shoddy treatment from others. They have little left to give to their children, and are more than likely to repeat the injury.

CATHY

When Cathy was small her mother had beaten her with an electric cord and locked her out of the house without shoes in the snow. But the event which she remembered most vividly was when her mother brought her a kitten for her very own. She carefully collected scraps to feed this small, warm, furry being, and slept with it next to her cheek at night. After a week, the mother decided the kitten was too much trouble and drowned it in a pail.

When Cathy was a young woman, she still felt helpless and frightened much of the time. She devoted herself to keeping other people happy. She cleaned the house, cared for her younger brothers and sisters, and worked as a nurse's aide. She dressed plainly, and never flirted. She shyly refused when a quiet young man who lived nearby invited her to a dance. She had decided that she was too clumsy to dance.

At age twenty, Cathy met Roy, a painter who had contracted to refinish the house. He asked for a cup of coffee and insisted on repaying Cathy by taking her out. Handsome, impulsive, and irrationally jealous, Roy soon monopolized all Cathy's free time. Her housework was left undone and her mother was furious. Caught between her mother and Roy, Cathy decided to elope. At least Roy seemed to care.

Marriage became a grim repetition of Cathy's early life. Roy was often unemployed and never helped around the house. So Cathy worked both at home and on the job. Roy accused her of having affairs with patients and occasionally hit her. He demanded that she respond in bed to prove her love for him. This requirement annihilated what little response Cathy could muster. She attempted to soothe Roy by faking a climax, by returning home immediately after work, and by never leaving the house without his permission.

Too frightened and depressed to separate from Roy, Cathy found herself pregnant. At first she was happy because Roy was more considerate, but by the end of her pregnancy her misery was compounded by swollen ankles and a huge abdomen. Labor commenced while she was at work in the nursing home. The call to Roy was unanswered, so she completed her duties, and at the end of her shift, took a bus to the hospital.

Alone and in pain, Cathy delivered a baby girl. Roy arrived the next day and expressed disappointment in the baby's sex. He presented her with a bouquet of flowers and announced that he was leaving with a construction crew shortly.

Three weeks later, Cathy was home with baby Mitzi awaiting word from Roy. Mitzi cried incessantly from late afternoon until early morning. Cathy fed her repeatedly. burped her, rocked and changed her, to no avail. Finally she called the hospital and was told to put the baby to bed. Mitzi continued to fuss, and Cathy became more and more upset. She shook Mitzi violently, and for a few moments there was silence. Then Mitzi began again, this time with a high-pitched whine like a cat's cry. Cathy suddenly lunged forward, snatched Mitzi and threw her against the wall, screaming, "I'll teach you!" Two hours later, Mitzi was dead.

Cathy was reared not in the slums, but in a privileged, middle-class neighborhood. Yet she developed the same helplessness, terror, and resentment as the women who lived in the high-rise apartment house. Cathy expected to be overburdened and victimized; her choice of a mate fulfilled these expectations. To ward off criticism and abuse, she strove to please everyone, thus eliminating her own needs as unimportant. Her fear, depression, and inability to accept passive pleasure severely compromised her sexual response, even before Roy commanded her to climax. Ordinarily, Cathy was a kind, responsible girl. Underneath lay rage which erupted into irrational violence when she could no longer please— Roy by bearing a boy infant, or Mitzi through soothing her suffering.

The link between anger and sex is even clearer when a woman such as Cathy marries a reasonable man. Such a choice is a fluke or an intellectual decision, as she commonly picks a cruel, fearsome, or rejecting male who will recapitulate her childhood. A few months after a more conventional marriage she becomes the wrathful, controlling, critical partner who abuses. She may withhold sex, prefer masturbation to making love, criticize her husband's technique, or openly take a lover.

DEBBIE

Wesley, his wife Linda, and their two children lived in a medium-sized town adjacent to a city. Wesley was a tall, neatly groomed, middle-aged man who had worked as a computer programmer for many years. His wife had served as an assistant librarian since her children entered school. Both were active in civic affairs, and Wesley was a deacon of the church. Although the couple seldom went out together, they would often have friends in for dinner. Both of the children did well in school, and Brian, the younger, had had a paper route since he was twelve years old. Debbie, now age sixteen, had begun piano lessons at age six and was capable of performing admirably in local concerts. In the summer, the family took trips and picnicked together.

Wesley and Linda admitted that their children had minor behavioral problems as they grew. These were handled without difficulty by Wesley, who was very firm in enforcing the rules. Corporal punishment had never been necessary except once when Brian had lied to his mother. On that occasion, Wesley applied the belt as generously as his own father had administered the razor strop. Brian stood to eat for a week, and never again lied to his mother.

Family members described their life together as completely happy. The only exception, perhaps, was when a neighbor at a coffee klatch asked Linda about her sex life. Linda seemed embarrassed and then said, "Well, I can't complain about it."

Debbie had not been allowed to date until age sixteen, and she had refused many invitations. Now, after her sweet sixteen party, an attractive boy from a good family had invited her to a school dance. The night of the dance Debbie was excited and happy. Much dinner-table conversation revolved around proper dating protocol, with Debbie both listening and participating. All agreed that she should return home by twelve thirty, a half hour after the end of the dance.

That evening, Wesley and Linda retired at ten thirty. Wesley, unable to sleep, rose to sit in the darkened living room. At twelve fifteen he was standing silently by the window which faced the lighted front porch. Debbie and her boyfriend paused on the top step and briefly embraced one another. Then Wesley observed his daughter laugh and snuggle against the boy's shoulder before parting.

As Debbie closed the door, Wesley seized her by the hair and slapped her furiously across the face. Debbie started to cry out, but her father hissed, "Shut up, slut!" and pushed her stumbling toward her room. After the door slammed, Debbie lay confused and sobbing on her bed. Several minutes later, the door opened and a man she hardly recognized as her father entered. Threatening to kill her if she called out, he tore her clothes and raped her, while calling her every vicious and degrading term he had ever known.

Although Wesley was absent from the breakfast table that Sunday, he did attend church. He didn't seem anxious or guilty. The crime was never discussed at the dinner table. Linda had heard the struggle but assumed that Wesley was disciplining Debbie. Debbie appeared quite depressed and refused to date until she left for college. She no longer sought her father's advice and responded minimally to his questions. Only Brian asked her what was wrong, and was upset when she began to cry.

Debbie entered analysis many years later. She had married an understanding, hardworking, but rather passive husband, who was perplexed by her sudden depressions and by her anger when he tried to comfort her. Eventually he ceased making sexual advances, as she would suddenly burst into tears. His loneliness and sorrow finally became so apparent to her that she sought help from a psychiatrist.

In therapy, she was unable to remember months or even years of her early life. As she became stronger she began to trust that her psychiatrist would not attack her. She remembered and reexperienced earlier events. She recalled reading while nestled in her father's lap and sitting beside him at church. She remembered how strong he seemed, and how much he was respected by others. In contrast, her mother was the one who worried about little things, who nagged and criticized for shoes left in the hallway or doors ajar. She complained of sick headaches but nevertheless kept the house spotless. Her mother expected extra cleaning chores from Debbie because she was a girl, even when Brian was out playing baseball.

Slowly, Debbie came to understand, if not forgive, her

father. She realized that his sudden rage stemmed from his rigid, puritanical background and the sexual deprivations of his marriage. She traced the gradual development of his intensely erotic feelings for her and appreciated his enormous effort to control himself. Her vivacity and warmth had been his most precious possession.

After many months of therapy, Linda no longer burst into tears at her husband's advances. It was not until a year had passed that she found words to encourage his sexual advances. At present, the relationship has become comfortable for both, but sexually satisfying only for Debbie's husband.

Encyclopedias have been compiled to list and catalog the distortions of sexuality. Each distortion shows a link between sex and another emotion such as rage or fear. The frightened exhibitionist unzips his fly in order to elicit anxiety in the observer, so he may reassure himself. The ascetic turns anger upon himself and denies all pleasure, but especially sex. The rejected husband may systematically have intercourse with a succession of different women whom he never intends to see again. A woman selects a jealous man to marry, and then provokes him. Whether in victim or aggressor, the link is present. It is firmly fused in early childhood and difficult or impossible to change. The only solution is prevention.

In order to prevent such links from forming, we as parents must do more than intellectualize. We must not cruelly inhibit, abuse, reject, abandon, or severly criticize our children. We must not bind them so closely that they cannot grow. But is there anything positive that we as parents can do? I believe there is.

11

KEEP IT IN THE FAMILY

Sex before eight or else it's too late.

—Slogan of the
René Guyon Society

MANY PARENTS AVOID DEALING WITH THEIR CHILDREN'S EROT-
icism because of conscious or unconscious fears of incest.
Many fathers recoil in dismay at a partial erection while
wrestling with a daughter, or—even more disquieting—with
a son. Yet children continue to rub, hug, and feel parents.
Parents react by limiting the amount and kind of contact.
They shun kissing children on the lips, remain fully clothed
when youngsters are about, and avoid prolonged physical
contact. Kissing becomes a conventional gesture—limited, predictable, and safe. This is necessary, at least for the comfort
of the parents.

Do early sexual experiences erode children's morals, increase criminal behavior, and promote indiscriminate lust?
These are commonly held assumptions. Data from other societies indicate that these dangers are grossly exaggerated. But
what of our own culture? The slum and the commune are
scarcely typical of our family structure. There is one event
that occurs in all strata of society and that provides young-

sters with intense erotic stimulation—incest. While incest can lead to serious problems, it is not always harmful. (Finch, 1973; Sarles; Yorukoglu, 1966; Rassmussen, 1934; Bender, 1952; Schlacter, 1960) A study of incest aids in our understanding of children's sexuality.

Incest taboos are the strictest and most ubiquitous moral constraints known. (Henderson, 1975; Murdock, 1949) They exist not only in human society but also in chimpanzee and monkey groups. For instance, male chimpanzees living in the wild do not copulate with their mothers. Brother and sister chimpanzees may mate with each other, but less frequently and less enthusiastically than with other chimpanzees. Father chimpanzees apparently do not recognize their offspring and may couple with their own daughters. (Jensen, 1972; Goodall, 1958) Human cultures are analogous in that only mother-and-son incest is universally prohibited.

Legends and plays have depicted incest throughout history. Marriage between brother and sister was not uncommon in ancient Egypt if the children were related only through the father. It was prohibited if the two were born of the same mother. Cleopatra was a product of a series of such incestuous marriages and eventually, in spite of Caesar, did marry her brother. Among the ancient Greeks and Hebrews, marriage among family members was permitted in order to conserve wealth and power. The Bible describes incest between Lot and his daughters after the death of Lot's wife. Salome had an incestuous relationship with her stepfather, who was also her uncle. In Greek mythology, Zeus married his sister Hera to produce a family of lesser gods. The legends of Oedipus and Phaedra warned of the inevitable death and destruction which would ensue after the rupture of the incest taboo.

Most cases of incest are never reported, and accurate statistics are not available. It appears to be most frequent in overcrowded dwellings and in isolated rural areas. (Lutier, 1972; Lustig, 1966; Weinberg, 1955) Alcoholism, poverty, retardation, emotional deprivation, and difficulties in sexual adjustment are also implicated. (Tormeys; Weiner, 1962) Immediate factors, such as the mother's absence, increase the likelihood of father-and-daughter incest.

According to Weinberg's study of 203 cases, 78 percent of incest occurs between fathers and daughters or stepfathers and stepdaughters. Eighteen percent is between brothers and sisters, and one percent between mothers and sons. The remaining three percent are multiple relationships.

Sibling incest is least often reported and is usually handled within the family. Incest between prepubertal children commonly follows a pattern of normal sex play, leading eventually to heterosexual intercourse with no particular emotional damage. Fox found that brothers and sisters who experiment together before puberty are *less* likely to be sexually attracted to each other after puberty. Recent studies of Israeli kibbutzim and of Taiwanese children also indicate that early social familiarity reinforces the incest taboo. Mutual sex play among siblings does not prove harmful, and could foster a robust, healthy, nonincestuous stance later in life. (Weiner, 1962; Riemer, 1940; Fox, 1962)

Mother-son involvement is the most malignant form of incest. Prohibitions against such relationships are the strongest of all. Raphling et al. describe a family where multiple incestuous relationships occur. The son who was the chief perpetrator of the liaisons is nonetheless disgusted by his mother's attempt to seduce him. He continues to bear resentment toward her. Mothers who seduce their sons have severe emotional disorders and are often psychotic. They may abuse alcohol and be promiscuous. The child is ordinarily left confused and angry, although Finch reports that one fourteen-year-old boy who had coitus with his mother for several years nonetheless maintains a good adjustment with many features of a healthy personality.

Between the near normal sibling incest and the highly

pathological mother-and-son incest lie the majority of cases. These are the father-and-daughter or stepfather-and-stepdaughter liaisons. The relationship usually exists for an average of three years prior to discovery. Occasionally molestations are reported immediately by a shocked daughter or her irate mother, but this is the exception. Many unions are never revealed. In the liaisons that persist the whole family is involved in a tangled conspiracy. All members of the family are aware of the activity but avoid acknowledging it. (Sarles, 1975; Poznanski and Blos, 1975; Kaufman, 1954; Riemer, 1940)

BARBARA

Barbara's mother was chronically tired and vexed by the father's inability to hold a steady job. She insisted that his snores kept her awake and suggested that he sleep on the top bunk of nine-year-old Barbara's bed. Barbara did housework and cooked her father's favorite dishes because her mother "couldn't stand the smell." Barbara was flattered when her father brought her special gifts and sought her opinion and advice. When her father's attentions became blatantly sexual Barbara complained to her mother. The mother called her a liar and a whore with dirty thoughts. Barbara no longer resisted and soon began to enjoy coitus. When she was twelve years old she asked her father for a ten-speed bicycle. Not only did she not receive one, but her father began to pay attention to Barbara's eight-year-old sister. Barbara was furious and the next day told her teacher everything. The police questioned the father and put him in jail. The mother vindictively accused Barbara of lying and attempting to break up the marriage. Barbara was placed in an experienced foster home. She was seductive toward her foster father until he gently but firmly restrained her. Next she became enamored of her English teacher and finally of a classmate. While in jail the father admitted the incest but asked for leniency because "I was afraid she'd get mad at me if I didn't give it to her."

Although parents are upset and under severe stress at the time of exposure, they seldom express guilt. (Poznanski and Blos, 1975; Sarles, 1975) Common rationalizations include: "It was my duty as a father to teach my daughter," or "I was afraid she'd get hurt if one of those bastards at school got her first."

What repercussions might we expect in the daughters? There are several patterns. If the daughter is cruelly coerced, especially if she is very young and in great pain, her perception of sex and her character will suffer. The following is from a court-ordered evaluation.

JANE

Jane appeared older than her fifteen years. Casually dressed in a sweater and jeans, she squirmed, giggled nervously, and blinked her long false eyelashes. Her incestuous relationship with her father had begun when Jane was only six years old. It continued uninterrupted in spite of her father's five successive marriages. At age fourteen, Jane became pregnant. Both she and her father wanted the baby. The father devised an ingenious scheme whereby he would hire a man to marry Jane and then divorce her. That way Jane would remain at home and the family's income would be augmented through county aid. Yet the father eliminated every prospective husband because he feared the man might take advantage of his conjugal rights. Finally the father married Jane himself under an assumed name. Jane inadvertently called him "Daddy" during the ceremony and then frantically corrected herself. The father was jailed, and Jane was placed in a foster home where, several months later, she gave birth to a nine-pound baby boy. The court requested my evaluation as evidence for her father's trial.

Jane recalled her initial coitus at age six. At first she had refused and wept bitterly. Her father had beaten her with a belt and Jane had submitted. In the years that followed, her hesitation provoked a punch with his fist or a whack with a board. Several years later Jane's young sister, Terry, joined Jane as the father's servant for sex. Terry had been beaten and ridiculed not only by her father but by the rest of the family as well. Each night the three would play a hand of poker—the loser was to tend father's sexual needs. Mysteriously, the father never lost. In spite of her anger, Jane became fully orgasmic before age ten.

As Jane matured she assumed a position of great power compared to the younger children. The father was less brutal with her and gave her special privileges. When a new stepmother entered the family, Jane insidiously belittled her, much to the father's amusement. No stepmother lasted for longer than two years. After the departure Jane would once again resume full command. When she complained about the younger children, her father beat them viciously. As Jane became a shapely young woman, her father jealously guarded her from the attention of her classmates. He arrived at school exactly three minutes before the last bell and solemnly escorted her home.

At the time of our interview, Jane's gravest fear was that her father would be freed. He would beat, perhaps kill her for revealing the truth. Although she and her foster mother were at odds, at least she could attend school while her baby was well tended. Now she openly dated boys and described several as "real foxy dudes."

Shortly after our interview Jane and her baby were removed from that home. The foster mother had intervened as Jane spanked her infant son for crying. Enraged by the interference, Jane had dumped a pail of dirty, soaking diapers over the foster mother's head.

Several months later, Jane was reevaluated while in her second foster placement. She was already incredibly hostile toward her foster mother, who was "trying to take over *our* baby." She never mentioned any boys her own age but longed to live again with her father, whom she portrayed as strong, caring, and smart. She had forgotten the beatings and was angry at the "crooked" police and social workers. Jane thought she should have sworn that two men raped her so that her father would not have been jailed. Shortly thereafter, Jane angrily ran away from that foster placement, abandoning her baby.

Somewhere, Jane awaits her father's release from custody.

When incest is forced amid tears and beatings, eroticism and anger become linked much as they did with Cathy in the last chapter. Yet Jane is fully orgasmic while Cathy's response was seriously impaired. Jane clearly describes intense early erotic stimulation, while Cathy was unable to recall any self-stimulation or sex play at all.

Incest is not ordinarily accompanied by brutality—seduction is the common route. Ready rationalizations by a respected father and enjoyable sensations pave the way. The young child who doesn't know that incest is immoral is both flattered and fascinated. It feels good and gets better with practice. Incest becomes a private game, a "secret" from the mother.

GLORIA

Gloria's stepfather was an Air Force sergeant who married a Filipino woman and adopted her two illegitimate children. Their marriage produced one additional child. The oldest girl, Gloria, was twelve at the time of the interview. Her stepfather had molested her since she was seven, beginning less than a year after his marriage.

Gloria's parents sat close together on the couch. The mother spoke rapidly in broken English, while the stepfather clarified and interpreted her statements. She was an excitable lady who complained of migraine headaches, sore throats, and nervousness. She depicted herself as an easygoing person who tried to forget troubles. She didn't see why the evaluation was necessary, and didn't feel therapy would be helpful. Both parents blamed the molestation on the stepfather's heavy drinking.

The mother never slept with the stepfather because she insisted on taking their five-year-old son to bed. The stepfather slept on the living room couch next to Gloria's bedroom. Gloria's door had never had a lock. The mother complained that the stepfather drank all the time and would approach her sexually by slapping and pinching her. She didn't like that kind of sex. When I inquired about the stepfather's sexual function he indicated that he had not performed "in quite a while but I think I still could."

Gloria appeared to be an attractive, mature young lady. Shy at first, she soon relaxed and spoke freely. For as long as she could remember, her stepfather would enter her bedroom at night to fondle her breasts, rub her genitals, and lie on top of her. He never attempted to penetrate her and never used force. She disliked the smell of stale gin but was aware of intense physical pleasure. At age nine she initiated sex play with boys in the neighborhood and enjoyed that also.

When Gloria was seven or eight, she told her mother about her stepfather's nightly forays. Her mother screamed at the stepfather until he retreated to the corner bar. Yet the mother continued to go to bed at eight, the stepfather still slept on the couch and there was no lock on Gloria's door. Three days later, the stepfather began again. Gloria persistently informed her mother. Finally, the mother told her to stop making up stories.

The final molestation occurred on an evening when the parents went to a neighbor's house to watch a "dirty movie." Gloria baby-sat with the younger children. The stepfather returned alone and intoxicated, fly already unzipped. He didn't expect the neighbors to follow.

Gloria was an A student and president of the Homemaker's Association. She contributed to the school newspaper and planned to become a nurse. She wished to live at home while she attended college. She had many friends and especially liked boys and soul music. She wanted to marry a man who would be rich, helpful, cute, and a good dancer. Her three wishes were for a car (a Firebird), jeans, and a million dollars.

Gloria preferred to remain at home in spite of the molestation. Yet she easily accepted the court's decision that she be placed in a nearby foster home. She visited her parents daily but always returned to her foster home before dusk.

Incest does not necessarily produce damage. Rasmussen reports on fifty-four women who had incestuous relationships between ages nine and fourteen. Forty-six are functioning normally in the community and seem unaffected by the experience.

The girls I have evaluated who were young, uncoerced, and initially pleased with the relationship remain emotionally unscathed, even after protracted incest. However, they may be devastated by the social consequences after discovery. They are fully orgasmic, sexually competent, attractive, and sometimes seductive. Guilt is a relatively late occurrence, often not appearing until early adolescence. When guilt does occur, it is nowhere near as shattering as when incest commences in adolescence. When these girls move out into school and the community, they swiftly form gratifying liaisons with more appropriate males. They retain a taste for older partners, such as foster fathers, male teachers, doctors, and policemen.

When assessed by a psychiatrist, a patient such as this displays a knowing smile, wears snugly fitting clothes, and seems more mature than other adolescents. On request, she sketches a person—unmistakably female, with rounded thighs and voluptuous lips. She has both the taste and the knack.

When the outcome is foster placement, the transition may require the relinquishment of pleasure. Society expects its children to be asexual and the foster home may be totally unprepared for a sensuous child. One social worker commented, "It takes an older couple with plenty of experience." In an understanding, unruffled placement the girls usually do adjust, temporarily inhibiting their eroticism as convention dictates.

Incest that commences in adolescence is different and devastating. Unlike the younger child, the adolescent girl has already comprehended and incorporated the moral standards of society. She admires her father and derives her moral values and self-esteem from the stability and mutual respect she perceives in the parents' relationship. The girl views her father's seduction as a traitorous act, a betrayal of her mother and of all women. If she feels pleasure she is debased and depraved. Profound guilt, depression, and helpless rage result. Fatigue, insomnia, headaches, and suicidal gestures occur and grades may drop precipitously. She may become compulsively promiscuous or refuse to date. Bitterness and frigidity may follow. (Sarles, 1975; Schlacter, 1960; Kaufman, 1954; Tormeys, 1972)

Although the daughters who experience incest early and without pain or coercion are not damaged by the act itself, incest remains symptomatic of major family pathology. Incest is considered immoral. It places the child in an abnormally powerful, yet vulnerable position. The girl takes precedence over her own mother but forfeits the warm, safe role of child. She may be possessed by a jealous father who restricts her from healthier outlets. She may be discredited, torn from the home, shunned by friends, and cross-examined in court. She may feel responsible for her father's jail term, for the family chaos, and for the divorce, if one takes place.

There is an important lesson to be learned from noncoercive father-and-daughter incest. Early erotic pleasure by itself does not damage the child. It can produce sexually competent and notably erotic young women. Childhood is the best time to learn, although parents may not always be the best teachers.

12

SEX AND SACRILEGE

TWENTY YEARS AGO, TO BE "FOR SEX" WAS TO BE AGAINST TRA-dition, the family, and the church—comparable to swearing at one's mother or wearing blue jeans to church. Times have indeed changed. Now we endorse gourmet eroticism with a spouse, although as a topic sex is still banned from polite conversation. Today, superstars announce bisexuality, and sex-change operations become an issue on the tennis court. Somehow, promoting children's eroticism is the worst yet. How far is too far?

There is a vast difference between foresight and hind-sight. Things that were murky are clearer in the retrospecto-scope. Every one of the men who engendered sociosexual change was perceived as an iconoclast at the time. Yet every one of these men was religious. For instance, Freud was con-demned as prurient. Yet Hunt described him as a "rather puritanical, romantic, and inhibited young man . . . chaste before marriage, devoutly monogamous after it." Freud sup-ported religion; he felt that it promoted refinement and was the best foundation for education.

The works of Alfred Kinsey provoked a similar furor. Yet in 1954 he wrote:

> This is the season [Christmas] in which many persons are re-examining their faith. I should, therefore, like to say again that my faith in men and women has steadily grown as I have

learned more about their history. Even though some of these histories have included things which did no good to anyone, and occasionally things which may have done outright damage to someone, most of the things which I have seen in the histories have increased my faith in the basic decency, the basic honesty, and the basic reasonableness of human behavior. . . .

I have found that the sexual behavior of most men and women, including even their most cantankerous and socially impossible behavior, makes sense when one learns about the handicaps, the difficulties, the disappointments, the losses, and the tragedies which have led them into such behavior. I believe that most people would exercise greater Christian tolerance of all types of sexual behavior, if they understood, as I have begun to understand, why people do what they do sexually.

Faith in God was not incompatible with the acceptance of human sexual behavior.

Masters and Johnson exploded the secrecy of sex when they recorded and analyzed the act itself under the glaring lights and cameras of their laboratory. This approach was shockingly antiesthetic. Sex was pragmatic rather than romantic, and again there were cries of sacrilege. Yet in 1975, Masters and Johnson wrote:

When a man and a woman first commit themselves to each other sexually they do so for reasons that have been impressed upon them by society since childhood. They have been led to believe that on the basis of their union they will find physical, emotional and social fulfillment—and some people would include spiritual fulfillment as well. These are dimensions of human needs that have been intricately woven into "patterns" for commitment; woven and rewoven by successive generations from concepts of love and sex which reflected prevailing religious and cultural philosophies. . . . Sex functions best when it is lived rather than performed and it can be lived best in a deep continuing commitment which is still most commonly a marriage.

All these researchers are committed to traditional values and see sex as primarily constructive rather than destructive. Of course, the road to hell may be paved with good intentions. The goal of heightened eroticism might also promote extramarital sex or in other ways erode the sanctity of the family. Here the sex clinics seem in opposition to organized religion. The clinics say that sexual fulfillment strengthens any union by providing a common base, a vehicle for intimacy, and communication. Christianity perceives coitus as permissible only in marriage and dangerous or damaging in any other context. In his syndicated column of November 26, 1976, Reverend Billy Graham responds to a mother who states that her daughter and her fiancé became of "one flesh." They asked the Lord's forgiveness for this sin, and now are no longer engaged. Would it be spiritually correct under the circumstances for her to marry any other man? Dr. Graham replies: "Your daughter has put herself in a precarious position. She compromised her ideals, lowered her moral flag, and thereby lost her boyfriend. What most girls don't realize is that sexual compromise, rather than drawing lovers together, usually drives them apart. Many a boy (and boys are different from girls in this respect) has as his goal total sexual commitment. Hence, when this is attained interest wanes." Dr. Graham holds that sex forces lovers apart and that sexual compromise sabotages intimacy. Yet one might be grateful that sex was not used like a carrot (or a cherry) on a stick to lure the boyfriend into a marriage for which he was totally unprepared.

The answer, as always, lies someplace in between. Sex is not a disease, nor is it a panacea for human misery. Those who feel ashamed of their bodies or guilty of a transgression against God may rupture a relationship because it "went too far." Other young people may, if they choose, use sex to extend or intensify an alliance. The decision is made not solely for passion but for a variety of conscious and unconscious reasons. If adolescents are comfortable with their bodies, they have a choice.

Sex doesn't deserve such notoriety. A natural function becomes a poison on one hand and an antidote on the other. Eroticism is the most fun but hardly the most significant or crucial of human needs. No one thinks of sex as the boat sinks, or even while elbowing through a mob at Macy's. Oddly enough, the unwarranted emphasis on sex is a Christian artifact. Sex must be powerful if it is equated with the devil.

The unwarranted power of sex was well illustrated by the controversy over bundling. Bundling was a custom encouraged in eighteenth-century Europe and colonial America, whereby fully clothed young couples shared a bed both to conserve warmth and to become better acquainted. David Mace reports that by the mid-nineteenth century bundling was described as a "ridiculous and pernicious custom" which "sapped the fountain of morality and tarnished the escutcheons of thousands of families." (Stiles, 1871) Bundling was both attacked and defended by devout Christians, depending on their interpretation of its purpose.

In the nineteenth century, emphasis on the evils of eroticism increased. The family would inevitably deteriorate if sex were not confined to the marital couch. Thus marriage became a barter of sexual privileges, and the constructive aspects of sexuality were lost in the shuffle. Even within marriage too great an interest in sex was a threat. *Sexual excess in marriage weakens the brain by gratification of animal passions. Animal propensities are strengthened by the disgusting habit of secret vice. Moral pollution causes the shipwreck of our race. Those who gratify the lust of the flesh cannot be Christians. Sensuality withers the desire for holiness.*

These horrendous preachings still color our perception of sex. Are we corrupted if we start too early or enjoy it too much? This simplistic overemphasis on sex detracts from more basic concepts such as intimacy, mutuality, accountability, and trust. Sexual appetite has little to do with the degree of commitment, although a total commitment does include sex.

Rather than dictating social change, the church is a part of the culture, sharing its .contradictions and vicissitudes. Today there is greater diversity and change within church and synagogue than there is in psychiatry. Hellfire is preached in the tent while the *Paulist Press* tells Catholics of a new morality in which adultery should be judged according to the principle of "creative growth toward integration." A. N. Franzblau describes the Catholic Church as still imposing the severest of sexual restraints on its faithful. Celibacy for religious orders, rigid prohibition of divorce and abortion, and restrictions on interfaith marriage persist. Masturbation is officially regarded as sinful. Yet the Catholic Church of today is far less austere than the Catholic Church of yesteryear.

Judaism endorses a more positive attitude. The Talmud promotes all forms of sex play between husband and wife and encourages wives to use cosmetics and ornaments to maintain their sexual attractiveness in both youth and old age. "Enjoy life with the wife that thou lovest" (Ecclesiastes) epitomizes the Jewish view of marriage and sex. Sex can be robust and openly joyous. In other areas, however, Jews may be as strict as Catholics. Abortion and intermarriage are strongly opposed, and masturbation is discouraged. But contraception is allowed. Even though Jews are far more lenient about divorce than Catholics, the divorce rate among Jews is quite low. The encouragement of sexual expression is not associated with the disruption of the family.

Franzblau indicates that as religions mature, they tend to approximate one another. All religious groups are now more relaxed regarding sexual expressions such as masturbation. There is an awareness of the breadth and importance of eroticism. The Christian sector is currently committed to sexuality as an integral part of the human condition. Religions are increasingly realistic, without forfeiting the emphasis on the integrity of the family. Heightened erotic enjoyment is not incompatible with most religious principles, nor with monogamy.

The church continues to provide much needed structure and direction throughout all stages of growth. Religion not only defines acceptable behavior, but provides role modeling, values, and exercises through which a child can identify himself as a valuable person. The church provides consistency and strength of purpose in a rapidly changing, increasingly ambiguous society.

Religions of tomorrow will be more sophisticated and realistic. Sex will decline in importance, to take its place among other essential values that contribute to the integrity and stability of the family. Sex and intimacy will no longer be confused, and religious leaders will devise methods of shaping both so that they may eventually be used to strengthen the marital bond. The harsh, punitive, guilt-ridden approach to sex will fade. Sex will be seen as inappropriate at certain times rather than sinful or dirty. Masturbation and sex play will be accepted as healthy parts of childhood. The concept of oneness with God will be extended to describe, on a lesser scale, the ability to fuse with another of God's products.

Mary Calderone reviews the changes in sex education in the schools over the past thirty-five years. Sex education remains the hottest item in the school curriculum. The joke about the little boy who requests a practical demonstration from his sex education teacher illustrates this controversy. Talking about sex may overstimulate youngsters. They may start to experiment, or begin coitus too soon. A class on sex may give them tacit permission.

Sex education has been present in the schools for more an thirty-five years. Early efforts were mechanistic, much e a class in anatomy. In the early sixties soaring teenage nereal disease, illegitimate pregnancies, and our increased knowledge of psychosexual development stimulated a searching reappraisal. A plethora of educational efforts filtered downward toward elementary school. Immediately, local communities reacted with petitions and political pressure. Sex education was undermining parental authority and corrupting the youth. Right-wing organizations and fundamentalist groups rose in anger. They were well organized, vociferous, and effective. The result was that the parent, who has little say about the "new math," now has the absolute right to deny the child sex education.

Sexuality is now recognized as another competence just as the ability to lead is a competence. Such competences develop throughout childhood, and to a great extent depend upon the child's opportunity to learn. Education in the school is important, but by itself totally inadequate. Basic concepts and attitudes are learned before the child ever reaches kindergarten. By then he may have acquired such a poor sexual self-image that the most expert guidance cannot heal the injury. By age five the child may be ashamed of his body, stating emphatically that the penis is dirty and should not be touched. The little girl may know that she is nicer and cleaner than boys—as long as she keeps her skirt pulled down.

Yet if any remediation is to be accomplished, the school is the place to do it, as sex is rarely discussed in most homes. Unfortunately, the teacher's upbringing is no different from the pupils'. Additional training for sex education varies from a weekend workshop to a full year at the master's-degree level. Many teachers remain anxious and uncomfortable with their own sexuality and are certain to transmit discomfort to their pupils. They may tenaciously cling to lists and diagrams, or overemphasize the dangers of venereal disease. Teachers are human also.

How can we make the most of a difficult and complicated situation when our tools are inadequate and we begin too late? First, not all teachers are emotionally ready to teach sex education. They need permission to refuse. Those who are truly comfortable need encouragement and special training. The number of pupils in the class needs to be limited so that the teacher can reassure and give specialized attention to the child who is anxious or reticent. Some pupils can explore only when given much time and patience. The child's misapperceptions and level of awareness need to be repeatedly assessed so that an individualized program can supplant the rigid format. Emphasis on feelings in discussion groups needs to replace the mechanistic presentation of facts, sometimes repeated ad nauseam each year. Who cares if the child can't name the structure which leads from ovary to uterus?

Rethinking of teaching programs and methods leads to more effective programs. At present, children are segregated according to sex so that they will feel free to ask questions. This may be true, but wouldn't it be more therapeutic for children to learn to speak about sex with members of the opposite sex? We may find that we were treating the teacher's discomfort, and communicating our own uneasiness to the children.

For their effectiveness to be maximized, programs must begin as early as possible, in kindergarten or nursery school. Special techniques and materials are necessary. The child of two to five learns best through play; the child of five to eight learns well through a combination of play and discussion. A boy doll with an expandable penis, and a girl doll with a soft, sized-to-fit vagina and a clitoris would aid the process. These could be available for free, unstructured play as well as demonstrations. The teacher's presentation would focus not just on how sex works, but on how good it feels. Group discussions can revolve about the children's real sexual experiences. The teacher would provide acceptance, offer encouragement, and clarify misconceptions.

The most we can expect from our schools is a diligent attempt at remediation. Prevention of sexual problems rightfully remains at home.

13

WHAT NEXT?

> Customs or social mores have also played a heavy controlling role simply by creating in the individual, from earliest childhood on, the profoundly disturbing conviction that he or she is somehow out of step, bad, abnormal, solitary, or degenerate for no matter what genital sexual behavior."
>
> —(MARY CALDERONE, M.D.,
> seventy-three-year-old great-grandmother,
> president of SIECUS
> (Sex Information and Education Council
> of the United States),
> and former director
> of the Planned Parenthood Federation

IF CHILDREN ARE ALLOWED AND ENCOURAGED TO EXPERIENCE erotic pleasure, won't they talk more about sex, experiment with each other, and begin making love at an earlier age? Of course they will. But the changes will scarcely approach earthshaking proportions. It has been more than two and a half decades since Kinsey first dared to study our sexual habits, yet only recently has a perceptible change in the onset of adolescent sex activity been noted. This is in spite of readily available contraception, abortions, parental permissiveness, sex education, and erotic movies. The decision to commence sexual intercourse is multidetermined. It depends upon the person's relationship to his parents, degree and kind of sexual responsibility, perceived sociocultural values, early experiences, religious background, and the availability of a suitable mate. No matter how freely a girl may discuss sex and entertain thoughts of an alternative life style, she is not likely to choose to bed with a boy early if she dislikes her father or if she fears all males. If we begin to encourage eroticism we may expect children to show more erotic interest and enthusiasm. They are likely to seek sexual outlets earlier. Whether this includes intercourse depends upon many factors. Many adolescents continue to defer intercourse until adulthood, or until they can feel really comfortable with the opposite sex. Masturbation is a reasonable, readily available substitute, and an important step in the enhancement of the erotic response. Fantasies of a more substantial union are a time-honored expedient, now more acceptable to the female.

Yet encouraging our children's erotic development is scary. It depends on one basic assumption: that sex (like vitamins) is constructive and desirable. If so, then we want our children to experience plenty of good, nourishing, healthy sex. This does *not* mean any and every kind of erotic experience, for some are highly destructive. Incest has emotional and social consequences. Sex to exploit or degrade a child is vicious. Restricting a child to quasi-seductive, subliminal sex in his own house provokes enormous rage. We need to protect our children, but not protect them out of the entire arena.

The incidence of adult sexual impairment is appalling. Only a fraction of those who need treatment can find and afford it. This needless waste results from our irrational expectation that a fully inhibited "nice" child should evolve, without encouragement or guidance, into a sexually competent, highly erotic adult. Sex clinics can treat dysfunctions, but only parents can prevent them.

No reasonable parent wants his child to suffer a sexual

dysfunction. Yet it happens again and again. Parents avoid, mildly discourage, or whitewash sex. The toddler sitting on his potty chair, tweaking his penis, is given a toy "instead." Other parts of the body have names, but the clitoris seems not to exist. The penis is for carrying urine, or for putting seeds in Mommy's baby bag, but not for feeling good. A happy, productive little girl shouldn't have time for masturbation. And nobody ever says anything nice about Billy's penis.

The child becomes acutely aware of the parent's embarrassment and lack of enthusiasm about sex. Shame is a wordless concept infused in the toddler. By age four it is obstinately fixed, to plague the adult with crippling anxiety or pervasive apathy.

During the past hundred years, we have advanced from clitoral cautery as a cure for self-abuse to studied indifference to the child's eroticism. Clearly this is not enough.

PART II

ENRICHING
THE CHILD'S
SEXUAL
RESPONSE

14

GETTING TO THE ROOTS

THE SEXUAL RESPONSE IS LEARNED, BEGINNING IN EARLIEST childhood. Parents can aid its development immensely by accepting and encouraging eroticism. The principles are explicit and easily grasped. The goals are the prevention of sexual dysfunctions and the enhancement of pleasure.

Some parents won't wish to change anything. Others have closed this book already, with a sense of mild revulsion. If you feel that encouraging eroticism is immoral, unwholesome, or against religious principles, this book is not for you. If you're certain that sex can erode the family, take over the child, or limit his achievement, then read no further.

If you elect not to change one whit, this doesn't make you a bad parent. The existing system is time-tested and safe. Sexual dysfunction is presumably not the worst that can happen. Should your child change faster than society itself, he may encounter stress. Both you and your child can be criticized. The decision isn't easy. Whatever the answer, it must come from within. The most important determinant is your assessment of your own sexuality, and whether you wish to give your child a richer erotic experience.

If parents disagree about the approach, and can't resolve their differences constructively, then eroticism can become a battleground and the child a weapon. Then the child perceives sex either as a source of power over others or as a liability. Either way, distortions occur, and the child loses. Attitudes of housekeepers, baby-sitters, grandparents, and others are important. Even the neighborhood is signicant. A liberal college community is more conducive to change than a small midwestern town. Yet important strides may be taken in even the most rigid setting. A father's stated approval of his son's penis or a mother's playful caress as she bathes her baby is unlikely to evoke criticism anywhere.

The first steps are taken gingerly. It's hard enough to be open about sex with a mate even when sex is an approved item on the marital agenda. With a small and impartial observer there are no guidelines and no way to predict his reaction. It's downright scary. A positive remark about the genitals or a pat and a smile are enough for a start. Most likely little Jenny will flash a disarming grin as she trots off about her business. Perhaps an opportunity will present itself when least expected. Todd's mother recounted a shopping trip with her four-year-old son. She glanced down to find Todd pushing at his crotch with a look of utter exasperation. A short while later he repeated the performance. She asked him if he enjoyed doing that. In a grumpy voice Todd complained that his "peter" kept coming up when he didn't want it to. Mother smiled and said that his penis had a "special magic" to stand up and feel good. Todd's eyes grew large as he stared at his crotch with new respect.

With my training in child psychiatry completed, I embarked on a number of court evaluations. One of the first cases involved a five-year-old girl who was suspected of having been molested by a sixteen-year-old neighbor. I felt anxious, as I had never before initiated a conversation about sex with a child. My patient, Erica, arrived with her mother in tow. She was a totally charming little girl, eager to play and quite willing to talk. If left to her own devices she would have spent the entire session feeding the baby doll or painting bright and gooey designs on large sheets of paper. Her play revealed nothing about a molestation and she met my initial queries with indifference. Obviously, I was the one interested in sex, not she. Or perhaps Erica was cloaking her fear, using her enthusiasm with finger paint to avoid discussing some terrible event. My questions became more specific. Suddenly I realized that Erica couldn't understand me—her words were different. With minimal urging, she taught me her vocabulary. Urination was, "s . . . s . . . s," defecation was "ca . . . ca" and the vagina was a nebulous cavity ensconced between the "belly button" and the "push hole." This talk about anatomy inspired Erica. She described a large bowel movement she had produced that morning. With obvious relish, she placed a baby doll on a potty chair and scolded him for going "poop" in his pants. The baby doll was her baby brother. This was normal play for a five-year-old, and I was tempted to conclude that molestation had not occurred. After all, wouldn't Erica be more upset if something had really happened? I was about to end the session when I happened to think that any police officer could have questioned Erica more thoroughly. Made bold by self-criticism, I took brush in hand and drew a male figure in profile, complete with a large, protruding phallus. Erica watched intently. "Did you ever see one like this?" I asked. "That looks like Tommy's 'squirt dickie' when he tickles me," was her reply. The rest was easy. It was a nice "squirt dickie," it only felt good, and Tommy always stopped when she wished. Tommy told her not to tell Mommy because Mommy would be mad. When I commented that her mommy and the police were worried, she said she had told Tommy not to do that anymore. I reassured her that feeling good was nice, but that it was right not to worry Mommy too. Later in my report I indicated that Erica and Tommy had been involved in normal, noncoercive sex play, and that Erica showed no sign of emotional damage.

Far from having been frightened or upset by my inquiry, Erica was relieved that someone understood and disappointed that she wouldn't see me again. Had I dealt with my own embarrassment earlier in the session, I would have had time to discuss other important matters, such as Erica's perception of her own genitals, and how she felt about her brother's penis.

Shame about sex takes several years to develop. Preschool children are usually relieved when an adult will talk about sex, as long as the adult doesn't have a hidden agenda. The willingness to share affords great comfort and encourages the child to explore his feelings and perceptions further. Older, school-age children are more suspicious. They wonder why the adult is suddenly interested. Perhaps they were seen experimenting with a friend in the bush or spied upon while looking at dirty pictures. What's the parent after, anyway? School-age children need reassurance and a matter-of-fact, casual approach. Special techniques will be described later.

The first attempt at really talking about sex may seem earthshaking to you but can be pleasurable and comforting for your child. Be prepared for some startling misconceptions. My first session with my own children was a revelation. My six-year-old thought that babies resulted from kissing. My five-year-old wondered if boys have to pull on their penis in order to start the stream of urine. My sophisticated ten-year-old had once assumed that girls had a retractable penis they pushed out at will, like a bowel movement. At first, the parent learns more than the child.

Parents who have been raised in sexually repressive homes may sense acute anxiety when they speak about eroticism. This can be inadvertently communicated to children by a slight frown, phrases rapidly repeated, a higher-pitched voice, or an insistence on learning the correct facts about sex. Children perceive the parents' ambivalence accurately and attempt to guess the reason. This then becomes a source of additional misinterpretations. Parents with this difficulty need to resolve their own anxieties in order to deal constructively with their children. Either individual therapy or the new sex therapies may alleviate the problem and enable a more positive approach.

Most of the chapters that follow recommend certain approaches or tasks designed to develop eroticism in the child. Some may seem distasteful or disgusting. No one exercise, or even series of exercises, is essential to the erotic health of the child. Elect only those suggestions which are comfortable for you. The others are valuable in initiating the rethinking and exploration of your own perceptions. Your attitude toward children's sex is crucial, and like it or not, you communicate that attitude to your children every day.

15

BUILDING BLOCKS

CHILD DEVELOPMENT IS LIKE BUILDING A HOUSE. THE BASEMENT is the most important, especially the cornerstones of the foundation. If this is well built, the structure resists stresses and strains, withstanding most environmental forces. Conversely, a minor defect in the foundation can cause continuing or recurrent problems.

Problems that would be inconsequential in an adult can permanently cripple the fetus or infant. For instance, a virus, an X ray, or a slight oxygen deficit in the unborn child can cause abortion, stillbirth, congenital defects, retardation, symptoms of hyperactivity, or autism. (Pasamanick, 1972; Knobloch, 1975) Less than optimal oxygen in the newborn can impair the organizational and perceptual functions of the brain for the rest of the child's life. Yet these same insults are of little or no consequence in the older child or adult. The younger the organism, the more vulnerable it is.

The crucial shifts in emotional growth occur early also. We are just beginning to recognize the tremendous import of the first few months of life, when each child demonstrates a characteristic feeling state. One infant is cranky, while another is placid. Colic, circumstance, the mother's ability to respond, and heredity all contribute to this emotional attitude which eventually colors the child's outlook on life. The irritable, upset infant may later perceive the world as frustrating, unpredictable, or threatening. His mother's ability to accept his body unconditionally and accurately sense his needs must certainly mediate toward a happier view of the world. A mother who rocks, soothes, and is sensitive to the infant's needs gives him every opportunity to develop a positive feeling state.

The older infant and the child must solve a series of problems. They must learn to relate to others, control themselves, and establish independence. Certain challenges arise at certain times as a function of growth itself. For instance, the infant who can't even crawl doesn't need to control his actions. But the toddler who can pull open drawers and climb out of his crib does need to control himself. The child who is capable of attending school must emerge from the protected home environment and make friends his own age. Movement from one stage to the next depends upon the child's abilities, adequate solutions to earlier problems, and parental support and guidance.

The sex drive is part of the child. It moves through well-defined stages too. Eleven-month-old Abby is beginning to navigate. Propelling herself enthusiastically toward a toy, she hits her head on a table. An agonized wail summons her father, who cuddles and soothes her. In his embrace she feels warm and sexy. Just seven months later Abby is an opinionated woman of the world. She refuses aid and haughtily declines her father's lap. Instead, she grasps her baby pillow firmly between her thighs and rubs until satisfied. Various questions such as "Why don't girls have a penis?" or "Is it all right to marry Mommy?" are characteristic of certain ages. The child needs to resolve each issue in turn in order to realize his full erotic potential. Feelings of inadequacy, shame, or resentment interfere with a favorable solution on any level. The focus of the child's eroticism also evolves in a predictable sequence. First it's the mother's breast, then the mother's face and entire body. Later it's father, a teddy bear, and other children. Next comes the little girl down the block, a teacher, a best chum, and finally appropriate members of the opposite sex. Horizons widen as the child grows.

Impairment at any developmental level has its effect; the earlier the impairment the greater the damage. For instance, the girl who never developed an erotic interest in her mother is hampered in forming sexual attachments to her playmates, or a pleasure bond with her husband. The twelve-year-old boy with a firm erotic foundation who is secretly enamored of his teacher is only temporarily shaken when she rejects his clumsy overtures. The foundation for the adult sexual response is well established in the first six years of life.

Our cat has four kittens. One spits, claws, and scrambles up the cardboard litter box. She dashes across the kitchen floor and hides behind the refrigerator. A second kitten likes to be held and mews when he hears the children. Two others eat, sleep, and play with one another. Mama cat seems to love them all—why are they so different? Kittens and children are a heterogeneous lot, each with certain innate qualities, or temperament. The child's temperament consists of certain well-defined, relatively stable attributes which have been traced from infancy by researchers such as Stella Chess. She describes nine components to temperament such as adaptability, intensity of reaction, and distractability. Altogether these nine elements determine whether the child will be easy or difficult to handle under most circumstances. Difficult children require skillful guidance, as any nursery school teacher can attest. Most parents do well with an easy, tractable child, while most are exasperated by a moody, resistant, difficult child. Both the child's temperament and the parents' adaptation to it influence the development of the erotic response, as the following cases illustrate.

CARRIE AND HANK

In an effort to sustain their faltering marriage, the Andersons produced two children in three years. Helen Anderson described her first pregnancy as one continuous evacuation due to an impossible combination of morning sickness and diarrhea. Carrie was born with high forceps after twenty-six hours of hard labor. She arrived "screeching like a banshee" and stained olive green by meconium (fetal stool discharged before birth). When her father first saw her in the hospital nursery, she squalled while other babies slept. Carrie's first year was marked by intermittent colic that abated in time for teething to begin. Nothing worked for long. Helen felt helpless and exhausted. She suspected her husband, Burt, of having an affair.

When Carrie was fourteen months old she was more manageable, although still moody and easily upset. Helen and Burt were learning to communicate through marriage counseling, and Burt spent more time at home. Several months later, Helen again became pregnant. She was pleasantly surprised when her nausea abated after the first two months. At eight months she remarked that this infant was gentle compared to Carrie. Labor lasted only six hours and the birth was rapid and uncomplicated. Hank cried briefly after delivery, then yawned and blinked as he was bundled off to the nursery. Thereafter, he ate and slept at regular intervals.

The next two years were turbulent. Violent quarrels and Burt's unpredictable absences heralded the end of the marriage. When Helen upbraided Burt, Carrie ran through the house screaming, "I hate you," while Hank slept soundly in his bed. Helen and Burt finally separated when Carrie was almost five and Hank was two. Although Carrie had never been close to her father, she sobbed uncontrollably when he moved to a distant city.

Helen and the children went to live with Helen's parents. Shortly thereafter Helen was hospitalized for depression. Carrie began cruising her grandmother's house in the middle of the night. She wet the bed, picked at her food, and complained that no one liked her. Finally the grandmother sent both children to live with an aunt. The grandmother described Carrie as "a handful" but said that Hank always minded. The only time she had spoken sharply to Hank was once when she found him playing with himself.

By the time Carrie was seven, the mother had recovered from her depression, completed business college, and was employed as a secretary. She and the children were living in a comfortable bungalow near an excellent elementary school. However, Carrie disliked the school, had few friends, and refused to walk there alone. Hank skipped all the way to kindergarten, where he was in charge of feeding the hamsters. After school he visited a retired cabinetmaker who lived nearby. "Uncle Ben" repaired his toys and shared his lunch. Even after the confrontation with his grandmother, Hank continued to masturbate at night.

Burt visited the children every six months. Carrie vacillated between excitement and tears. She demanded his attention and scolded him for being late. Hank looked forward to his father's visits and placidly accepted his departure.

When Carrie was nine she was treated at a mental health center for anxiety and school phobia. The therapist discovered that Carrie had assumed that her father left the family because she was a bad girl. She tried and tried to be good, but something always went haywire. She inevitably said the wrong thing when she was upset. She had avoided any sex play because that was part of being bad. She knew that Hank did things like that, but he was "always good, anyway."

Carrie was a difficult child. Even under the best of circumstances, she would have presented problems. Her moodiness and hasty reactions contributed to continual upset. Hank's early experiences were just as frightening, but he was admirably equipped to cope with stress.

Difficult children don't always have emotional problems. The majority grow to be happy, stable individuals who understand and deal with their own uncertainties. In large part this is possible because of flexible, reasonable parents who provide both warmth and guidance to very special children.

MICHELLE

Michelle was the third of five children. Her mother waggishly described her as a "holy terror" from the time of birth. At age eighteen months she was impossible. Rambunctious and obstinate, she was gleeful or grumpy. Reasonable discipline provoked fits of screaming. Her mother finally controlled her either by diverting her attention or by holding Michelle immobile on her lap. Although the mother toilet-trained the other children at thirteen months she delayed Michelle's training until age two. Then Michelle understood easily but complied only sporadically. At age twenty-six months Michelle produced a large bowel movement while sitting on the lap of the vice-president of her father's company. Although her mother was furious, she merely apologized and whisked Michelle off to the toilet.

Finally toilet-trained at two and a half, Michelle was placed with a baby-sitter four days a week while her mother studied at a nearby university. Mrs. Grey, the sitter, had been well recommended. Her house was tranquil and neat, even when she cared for six active preschool youngsters. She insisted that the children pick up their toys, learn their manners, and speak quietly without interrupting adults. After several weeks at Mrs. Grey's, Michelle listened closely to her mother's instructions also. Yet she seemed sullen and irritable. Mother spoke to other parents who employed Mrs. Grey. They reported many benefits and no emotional problems.

After two months, Michelle was worse. She seldom smiled and no longer asked to be taken to the park. Mother decided to visit Mrs. Grey's for a half-day session. Within the first hour it was evident that Mrs. Grey had a mission to train children correctly. She adhered to a rigid schedule and was quick to cite any infraction. Her voice revealed intense anger at an insubordinate child. Obedient children were plied with cookies, stories, and play materials, while disobedient youngsters sat in the corner.

Over coffee, Mrs. Grey listed her child-rearing principles. Any improper behavior was due to the parents' laziness or stupidity. Michelle had "come around" pretty well and Mrs. Grey gave pointers on how to maintain that improvement at home. No child in her charge had ever shown any interest in sex except one little boy from a "dirty family." Since his mother was divorced, he must have been seeing "bad things" at night, which caused him to cradle his crotch whenever Mrs. Grey sat him in the corner. The more Mrs. Grey scolded him, the firmer his grip became. Finally, she told his mother to take him elsewhere—her only failure in fifteen years.

Michelle was transferred to a day-care center. After two weeks she was so enthusiastic that she forgot to kiss her mother good-bye. She was again an impulsive, distractable, but often delightful child. At home she once more played with the older children and tested every household rule.

When company arrived, Michelle knew that her parents couldn't pay much heed to her. Her favorite trick was to wander nude through the living room. She delighted in the guests' bemused stares and her parents' embarrassment. Expecting that Michelle would grow out of it, her mother paid no attention. Michelle undressed faster, more frequently, and embellished her performance with grotesque postures, protruding her bottom toward the guests. Exasperated beyond permissiveness, her father marched Michelle to the bedroom and forbade her reentrance until she was both clothed and polite. A subdued Michelle reappeared in time for dinner. Several days later her mother suggested a Saturday morning play session where Michelle and a four-year-old neighbor boy could romp naked in the backyard under the lawn sprinkler and smear one another with mud. When the two were utterly exhausted she hosed them down and returned their clothes.

Although Michelle had made good progress in kindergarten, her teacher wondered if she were mature enough for first grade. She promoted Michelle on the strength of the first-grade teacher who had dealt successfully with other difficult children. Michelle did surprisingly well. Although still moody and easily upset, she was in the top reading group and had several close friends.

Michelle was a difficult child blessed with sensible parents, who individualized their approach to suit Michelle's temperament. Michelle required greater patience and empathy than the other children. Her parents adjusted their expectations and protected her from situations which she was unable to handle. They helped her to control her own behavior without forfeiting spontaneity or pleasure.

Difficult children are likely to have problems, including sexual conflicts. Even easy children encounter major hurdles such as illness, divorce, or irresponsible parenting. Some teachers are rigid and some children hyperactive. Some parents are trauma for children, and some children are trauma for parents. How can the sex drive survive? If, in spite of all vicissitudes, the child perceives his genitals as pretty and pleasing in the first six years of life, his sexual response will remain healthy in spite of other, sometimes serious, emotional problems.

The next four chapters are devoted to developing the child's erotic foundation.

16

INFANT STIMULATION REVISITED

The mother of a four-month-old infant sighs, "It certainly will be nice when she can *do* more things." In fact, the infant under six months is doing a great deal. The brain expands at a phenomenal rate, becoming infinitely more complex as the baby makes sense out of no sense. Leboyer was the first to emphasize the importance of an early erotic experience. A gentle delivery, warmth, support—even music —can promote eroticism at any age. The infant smiles—and for good reason. Pleasant feelings differentiate later to become genital sensations and a need to be close.

How can parents help this process along at home? Most mothers and fathers instinctively handle the young infant with care. In this culture the mother serves as the primary parent, although fathers could fulfill the role just as well. Yet even concerned, responsible parents differ vastly in parenting style. One mother mechanically slaps on a fresh diaper while gossiping on the telephone, the receiver pinched precariously between shoulder and cheek. Another babbles to her three-month-old, knowing full well the baby can't understand. A third combs her infant's hair, and carefully places a bow on the topmost wisp. A fourth wraps hers like five pounds of salami and bundles him off to the sitter's. Her handling is abrupt and very firm. As she rushes toward a deadline, she may smell different also. Each of these infants receives a characteristic pattern of stimulation, and comes to perceive the world in different terms. Impersonal mothers yield children who don't get too close. Frighteningly efficient mothers may produce bumbling youngsters. Mothers who parade their best-dressed children in order to be praised rear offspring who value appearance. Mothers who are erotically involved with their infants raise sexy children.

Erotic parenting means the time and ability both to give and receive pleasure from the infant. This includes the attainment of body intimacy, which means the acceptance and enjoyment of all the infant's bodily functions and products. Sexual strivings must be recognized and encouraged, just like any other vital function. To do this the parent must first welcome the child as a sensual being. The parent who nuzzles, cuddles, and rubs not only soothes the infant and promotes an attachment but also develops the child's erotic potential. The application of delicately scented and delightfully creamy lotions to the genitals isn't just for hygiene or, as the label indicates, to protect against harmful bacteria. Lotions and oils are highly sensuous and the genital contact distinctly erotic.

What difference does it make anyway to call a spade a spade? After all, good mothers have always patted and powdered the penis and swabbed the clitoris. Haven't children always received sexual stimulation? They have indeed—along with many a mixed message. One mother rubs away until an erection occurs—then she avoids the penis and pins on the diaper. A father blows bubbles in his son's navel until the ecstatic infant produces an erection. The father stops. When a six-month-old pushes her rubber ducky into her crotch, the plug is plucked from the tub and she's swept off in a towel. Genital contact is strictly in the service of hygiene, indeed an asexual concept.

The term "infant stimulation" illustrates our need to see

babies as asexual beings. "Adult stimulation" immediately brings to mind erotic movies or secluded trysts. An erotic device, the vibrator, is known as a "stimulator." A thousand coital accouterments are to "enhance stimulation" and sex manuals expound on stimulation techniques. Not so "infant stimulation," which is a nationwide, well-funded program designed to promote the baby's cognitive skills. The infant is provided with toys to manipulate and crib mobiles to develop eye-hand coordination. The focus is everywhere except on the genitals. Applied to infants, "stimulation" becomes a term devoid of any erotic connotation.

Body intimacy is the key to earliest erotic development. At no time is the individual more open to feel or less inclined to censure than in infancy. The baby's whole body is a sexual organ. The joy of being held and caressed is fully appreciated in the first year of life. The kinesthetic delight of being swooped up in a parent's arms is learned and may later be revisited by making love on a swing. The free palm of the suckling infant which massages the other nipple, or a button on mother's blouse, contributes to the worldwide significance of a fingertip placed in the palm of a hand. The infant who inhales its mother's smell while lustily nursing is paving the way for what the French recognize as the greatest of all erotic enhancements—the scent of a beloved.

There are certain exercises that enrich the experience of body intimacy—for both mother and child. These are designed for use in the first six months of life. The first exercise may be begun on the delivery table, if the mother is alert, without pain, and has chosen an empathic obstetrician. The father can also share in the experience. This is the time to claim, acknowledge, and begin to enjoy an amazing, if often perplexing, being. A Tahitian mother first sniffs her newborn, and a mother even in our aseptic culture can distinguish her infant in the nursery by smell. At first your baby's scent is mixed with yours and a smorgasbord of other odors: the amniotic fluid, perhaps meconium, and all the Zephiran and alcohols of the delivery room. Altogether, a stimulating and highly erotic mixture. After catching his scent, touch the silken skin, gaze into his eyes, and enfold the tiny form in your own natural curve. Skin-to-skin contact is highly desirable, but sometimes inconvenient in the delivery room. You may taste your infant also. He's a bit salty, and not at all unpleasant. Unfortunately, both the smell and taste of birth are soon to be swallowed forever by a sudsy ablution in the nursery. Another article may vanish also—the foreskin. Some mothers who have borne several boys have never seen an uncircumcised penis because the operation is performed before the baby leaves the delivery room. So check *all* the vital parts.

Occasionally, a mother finds the baby's smell unpleasant or even disgusting. This is a danger signal which, if unresolved, severely limits the pleasure she can receive from her infant. In turn, this restricts the erotic and other joys that the infant gains from her. Closeness with another is impossible if the other smells bad. If the scent seems dirty, the mother is likely confusing sex and dirt. Sometimes a new mother who is frightened, drugged, or in pain is unable to perceive anything pleasurable. Another may experience the smell as unpleasant because she isn't prepared for the dramatic and irrevocable changes which motherhood conveys. It's a favorable sign if, after a day or so, the baby begins to smell pleasant.

Mothers on the delivery table who have the chance but avoid looking at the penis or clitoris are dealing with significant sexual inhibitions. Often such mothers say, "They'd think I was crazy" or "They told me it was a girl so I didn't need to check." In truth, they're embarrassed. They can easily claim and enjoy the other ninety-five percent—but the penis? Many a new mother carefully counts fingers and toes but leaves a more valuable appendage unowned and dark within the blanket. Mothers who retreat from the sight of infant genitals need to pay close attention to the next exercise.

There's time to concentrate at the first feeding. By now, the mother is comfortable and ready to assess not only the baby, but her own reactions. Unwrap your newborn and remove the diaper. The umbilical stump may seem bloody or black, but no matter. Look at the arms, the legs, the belly, and the genitals. All deserve careful attention. The clitoris may be hidden or covered with a mucous jelly. Two fingers spread the labia to reveal the contours. The newborn girl is still affected by your hormones so that the labia are flushed and the clitoris enlarged and glistening. Can you touch it? Is it any the less important or more frightening than the rest of the body? If your little boy has an erection can you gaze at it and feel proud? Is this the same pride you feel when he roots for the nipple, connects, and lustily sucks? Aren't both faculties valuable? Does his penis match your expectations? Is it bigger or smaller than anticipated? If the penis is uncircumcised slide back the foreskin to reveal the glans. In Mangaia, the circumcised penis is described as "having no hat." In effect, when you pull back the foreskin, you remove the hat to reveal the rosy-tipped, smooth, and shiny glans. Are you reluctant to touch it? Some mothers are so frightened that they never retract the foreskin. Eventually it adheres to the glans and often becomes infected.

Parents who avoid looking at, touching, and approving of the infant's penis or clitoris are also limited in relishing and encouraging their mate's sexuality. It's not only mothers who are constrained. During the hundreds of births in which I either officiated or observed, fathers were often present in the delivery room. Not once did a father initiate the checking and claiming process, although many mothers did. Neither mothers nor fathers closely examined a baby girl's clitoris, although I suspect some mothers did so later.

More advanced exercises involve your reactions to your infant's secretions. The first stools are composed of meconium —gray, green, and greasy like Kipling's Limpopo River. The majority of mothers gingerly swab it away as an unpleasant but temporary necessity. Smear it, and you'll find the consistency of finger paint with a distinctive and not unpleasant odor. The breast-fed baby's stool isn't difficult to enjoy. It has a flowery scent that adds spice to the diaper change. Body intimacy with your infant is based upon an unqualified acceptance of, and communication with, all of his body and its products. The glistening modicum of saliva or the dab of mucus which slips from the baby girl's vagina are bits of a cherished being, until recently a part of you. Full acceptance of these secretions is the same as the ability to savor your mate's sexual perspiration, semen, and saliva. Reluctance or revulsion in either erotic dimension connotes problems in the other. (Rogawski, 1976) Happily, growth in one also promotes growth in the other. Many a mother who habitually avoids touching her mate's penis is able to relearn after the birth of a son, thus attaining a deeper level of body intimacy in bed. Almost every new mother becomes more comfortable as the months progress. If you begin by changing the diaper with operating room precautions, you may end by unceremoniously scraping the stool from the cloth with one hand and flipping it in the toilet.

It's true that no human mother achieves the intimacy with her infant that a mother dog accomplishes with her pups. She licks, sniffs, and lies for hours while they suckle or sleep nestled next to her skin. She often eats the placenta and routinely cleanses the genitals with her tongue. Yet the attainment of body intimacy in the human is based upon the same five senses: hearing, seeing, touching, smelling, and tasting. Of these, the latter three, the near receptors, are the most primitive and meaningful, for they entail closeness or body contact. Yet these are the ones we avoid with cribs, bottles, clothing, high chairs, and propriety—all the accouterments of civilization. Adult eroticism is defended against in the same fashion, by night clothes, deodorants, and aversions to certain forms of foreplay. The prohibitions against watching or listening to another sexually attractive individual are weak compared to the injunctions against touching, smelling, or licking that person. Yet all senses must be involved in total body intimacy. This, in fact, is the only way that the baby comes to value a profusion of stimuli. If infancy passes without an abundance of these intimate sensations, then the sexual response will be limited. Thus all forms of licking, washing, tickling, and sniffing contribute to the growth of the eroticism. The mother who achieves body intimacy also provides her child with solid acceptance. The infant comes to feel valuable, through the experience of unconditional acceptance.

Breast-feeding is a potent gratification, for both mother and child. Rhythmic sucking, scent, warmth, and closeness combine to produce the optimal erotic congress. Genital pleasure is enmeshed in the total experience. Direct genital stimulation occurs as the mother presses the child's hips against her body. Many older infants spontaneously augment this by recurrently flexing their thighs. Anticipatory squirming and wriggling against the bedclothes and the undulations of the mother's body as she breathes, heighten the effect. Erections and vaginal lubrication are common. The mother receives pleasure through the repetitive tugging at her nipple and the tingling when the milk is forcibly ejected. This erotic reciprocity cements her attachment to the baby. Yet few mothers nurse and even fewer permit themselves to savor the experience. An occasional mother will report multiple orgasms and some describe a pervasive tranquillity similar to that which follows good sex. A graduate student compares suckling to a transcendental state of acute awareness where the body's boundaries dissolve. These sensations may be frightening also.

Bottle-feeding diminishes the opportunity to smell, taste, and touch one another; the mother receives less gratification and therefore the infant is more of a burden. Attachment is sometimes impeded. Yet with forethought, a large measure of body intimacy can be achieved. Skin-to-skin contact at feeding is essential, not only for the warmth and touch but because the scent is irreplaceable. Stroking, cuddling, and time to savor each other builds mutual satisfaction. If these suggestions are followed, the bottle-fed infant forfeits little erotic pleasure, although the mother still forgoes a lot. Breast-feed if you can.

Erotic growth in the first six months is based upon passive sensual gratifications. The infant is magnificently receptive, spiritually naked, and immensely vulnerable. Stroking, rubbing, and sucking are central to his existence. He must receive a variety of pleasures if he's to become a fully receptive adult. An adult who hasn't accomplished this or who tries to defend against passive receptive longings is treated in the sex clinic by tasks designed to develop his "sensate foci." He's told to relax completely while his mate rubs, licks, strokes, and nuzzles. He relearns a developmental task of the first half year.

A passive pleasure seldom allowed is for the infant to sleep in skin-to-skin contact with mother. Enveloped by her scent and warmed by her flesh, the baby is supremely stimulated. Instead, infants are put to sleep in cribs or cradles because the baby needs his rest, and because the mother needs time for other chores or because she might roll over and smother him. Perhaps the youngster couldn't easily be "broken" of the habit. These perils are vastly overrated. They arise from various unstated fears, especially that of an erotic involvement with the child. In many other countries, infants always sleep with mothers. They aren't smothered or emotionally warped. Older infants and children do need to individuate from mother. If they're confined and stimulated, harm can result. Not so the infant under six months, whose primary task is to receive fully a spectrum of erotic experiences. The greater the range and complexity, the greater the potential for pleasuring as an adult.

The mother or father who fears smothering the infant can

still lie skin-to-skin while listening to music, reading, or simply relaxing. If sleep intervenes the partner can assist by keeping watch.

Next to smell, touch is the cardinal sense of the young infant. As with any other receptor, it's developed only through a diversity of contacts. Touch can be light or firm, tickling or teasing, prickly or tingling, soft or breezy. The infant who experiences touch as only a tight swaddle forfeits the pleasure of delicate manipulations. A fine way to start this exercise is naked, together in the sun. If climate or closeness to neighbors forbids, a fur rug or fuzzy blanket beneath a warm lamp will do. Nuzzling, mouthing, and licking constitute a basic massage, common to all mammalian parents. Tickling and teasing are distinctly human. Apes, monkeys, and some underprivileged humans add grooming and nitpicking (in the literal sense) to the basic armamentarium. Grooming, whether by tongue or washcloth, remains an excellent erotic vehicle. Follow your inspiration, providing for your own pleasure and comfort as well. Intimacy is a process of both giving and receiving. Wallowing in warmth and closeness can be delicious for both. Rub the baby's skin with a rough terry-cloth towel, or slide him across a satin comforter on his belly. Amplify these sensations with a feather duster or blow gently with the warm air of a handheld hair dryer. Eyelashes impart an exquisite tickle and suds or bubbles which pop on the tummy tease and titillate.

Some say that the delights of water are first encountered in the uterus. Perhaps so, but the uterus scarcely provides the diversity of pleasure found in the bath. Warmth, bubbles, and the texture of water all combine to yield an experience second only to nursing at the breast. The infant creates a splash with the least effort, and the greatest sexual organ of all, the skin, is stimulated all over by the towel. A peak occurs as the genitals are soaped, swabbed, and rubbed with a soft cloth. The parent's touch and smile are captured in the total imagery.

The mother who focuses on hygiene as her raison d'être sacrifices a measure of body intimacy. She tests the water temperature with her elbow, immerses the infant, scrubs, rinses, and completes the cycle by plopping her charge in a towel. The pleasure she derives stems from her own efficiency rather than from her infant. She allows her baby no time for passive pleasuring.

Many an infant-grown-up snatches a stereotyped four-minute shower, grabs a towel, and proceeds about his business. As you may suspect, a task at the sex therapy clinic is for the couple to take a leisurely bath together, soaping and rubbing one another with a soft sponge.

As the infant's whole body is a sexual organ, each area needs to develop its full erotic potential. The genitals are ordinarily stimulated, if only under the guise of hygiene. The male infant rapidly learns to anticipate penis pleasure. He parts his hips and gazes at his mother in avid anticipation as she unpins his diaper. By the time the diaper is off, his penis is erect. The female infant reveals her excitement through rapt attention and vaginal lubrication. In contrast, the mother describes the diaper change as her least entrancing chore, a necessary but unpleasant duty. This attitude is reflected in her facial expression, her voice, and the quality of her touch. The stool smells and must promptly be discarded. Another diaper must be pinned in place to avoid an "accident." These anxieties limit the experience of body intimacy, and will, in the second half year, be perceived by the infant as dissatisfaction with his genitals. The assembly-line mother who approaches diapering like Rosie the Riveter not only suppresses eroticism but conveys resentment. Her infant-grown-up may well show an affinity for the bedcovers.

Diapering is prime time for the enhancement of genital eroticism. If the mother can feel pleasure and transmit enthusiasm as she swabs and dabs, the prognosis is excellent. She has at her disposal a myriad of scented lotions, oils, and powder to expand the sensitivity of the entire genital and rectal area. Textures such as cotton, terry cloth, and Baby Wipes provide enrichment.

Millions of infants in this world are reared entirely without diapers. The baby is simply suspended over the dirt by a mother who accurately reads his body cues. Genitals are subject to casual stimulation, such as rubbing against the mother's hip, licking by a friendly puppy, or tweaking by another child. Genital manipulation is often an accepted method to calm an irritable infant. Although statistics aren't available, sexual dysfunction seems far more likely in countries where diapers are employed. Certainly the parent who conceals the baby's genitals beneath a tightly pinned diaper assumes a huge responsibility. This parent becomes the infant's main source of genital pleasuring.

During the first half year, passive pleasures have dominated the scene. A feeling state has been established which will color not only the sex drive, but all other drives as well. The infant has been, and remains, monumentally egocentric, living only for himself. The division between mother and child, outside and inside, is hazy at best. Yet this has been the first golden age of eroticism, of complete and unqualified absorption in pleasuring. With the baby's ability to move about and manipulate toys, passive gratification becomes less prominent in the second half year.

During the second six months the infant develops a separate self and recognizes the parents as distinct individuals. Tears flow when the mother leaves, and there is obvious relief when she returns. The baby can now tolerate minor frustrations without appearing devastated. He can wait to be fed as long as he trusts that his mother won't forget. This favorable expectation is built upon the repetitive, predictable gratifications which the mother has provided in earlier months. Although body contact remains immensely important, the baby can wait to be picked up, rocked, or bathed. A modicum of frustration is healthy, for it helps the child to individuate. Prolonged body contact such as sleeping together is no longer necessary. The infant with a background of pleasure knows what he likes and now begins to seek that which feels good.

Elise is charged with boundless energy as she crawls about the room. She insists on the absolute possession of her mother's lap. She gives little thought to the presence of company as she snatches at her mother's blouse with obvious intent. While sucking, she grasps and releases the other nipple, rubbing the surface until it's fully erect. She's far more of a threat to her mother's sense of propriety than she was just three months before. Fortunately for her mother, Elise has other interests almost as attractive as the breast. Active pleasures like pulling pots out of the cabinet compete for the spotlight.

Since age five months Elise has bounced in a canvas swing suspended from a doorway. Now she has a walker and a rocking horse. These are her favorite toys. They keep her quiet and content for long periods. As she bounces and strains she provides herself with a genital massage. Small wonder she remains enthralled. Now she's able to construct sensation all by herself—a happy event.

Other babies discover different methods. Some little girls rub against a pillow or squeeze thighs together to create erotic feelings. The father becomes a playmate with a bouncy knee. As the world widens, passive pleasures are less enticing. A seven-month-old weans himself from the breast because he can't remain quiet long enough to nurse. He squirms and wriggles until barely satiated, then slides away to pursue the cat.

Parents can aid the acquisition of active pleasures by providing a variety of materials and the opportunity to use them. Time alone without diapers invites genital exploration. Most infants will at least feel their genitals and appear pleased. Those who miss the area in the first session are likely to discover it another time. If the mother is present when the genitals are appreciated, it's important for her to smile and demonstrate approval. Infants who neglect the penis or clitoris completely aren't failures. Each child enjoys a spectrum of unique and appropriate pleasures. More advanced exercises include the provision of large soft or fuzzy dolls and pillows of various shapes. The session can be extended to include play with mud or finger paint in the backyard or tub. If the mother can join in the smearing without concern for dirtying her hair, so much the better.

The infant in the second half year needs to develop reciprocity. In earlier months, the baby has lived within himself, with little understanding of his impact on others. Now the infant knows his mother and can actively return her attentions. A healthy reciprocity is essential for sexual and other relationships.

There are many kinds of reciprocal relationships: The mother demands and the baby acquiesces; he pleads and she nurtures; she cries and he gets angry. The kind of reciprocity which promotes wholesome sex is one of mutual give and take. These simple games for the older infant promote healthy reciprocity. The first is to blow forcefully in a hollow of the infant's skin, as below the neck, under the arm, or into the navel. This results in a flatuslike explosion and a delightful tickle. The infant is encouraged to reciprocate in kind. Don't expect too much, for this is a complicated sequence. Most infants will push or lick the parent and make a noise. Most essential is the parent's reaction—one of exaggerated delight. The infant feels proud and potent, having created pleasure in another, most important, person. Feeding one another is a game which demands the mother's mimicry for full effect. Splashing each other in the bathtub or tickling and scratching one another while lying on the bed are additional exercises. With a little imagination, you can devise a dozen other games.

Separation from the mother is scary for the older infant. The mother has always responded to his needs and soothed his misery before, but now when the door closes, all is over.

He's tiny, helpless, and utterly impotent. These feelings are understandable, but if they persist they will inevitably impede his erotic response. The man who feels impotent either fulfills that role or expends enormous energy proving otherwise. The woman who feels impotent gives up easily and is afraid to explore or ask for what she needs. Thus, potency needs to be cultivated from infancy on up, every step of the way. For the infant who's first experiencing separation, games such as "Peek-a-boo" and "Bye-bye" build confidence and provide gratification. In "Bye-bye" the mother waves and pretends to leave. In seconds she reappears to scoop her babe in a giant embrace. Next it's the infant's turn, while the mother asks petulantly, "Where's my baby?" The reunion is equally joyful. "Peek-a-boo" is a simpler version, using the hands or a blanket. Again the infant's active participation is vital. For a moment, the helpless child is transformed into a magician or commanding general—an experience in potency.

Teaching the infant to swim has been in vogue for a number of years. Initially these programs were sold to the public as the stylish acquisition of an essential skill. "You, Mother, can have the only infant on the block to swim twelve feet without taking a breath." Of course these expert tadpoles lost that ability if they didn't continue to swim. They learned again at a later age. The real payoff from infant swimming has nothing to do with skill. A wet, wriggly, naked body, ecstatic in the sensuous delights of water and the defiance of gravity, is hard to resist. Make the most of it. The basic format is similar to "Bye-bye." The instructor supports the little girl some feet away, while mother holds out her arms. The infant swims to her enthusiastic embrace. The child can scarcely contain her joy; she's done something great. As she clasps her thighs about her mother's waist, clitoral impressions add to her gusto.

Can the infant receive too much stimulation through these activities? Will eroticism take over the child? Data from many cultures yields an emphatic "no." Sexual enthusiasm and activity don't lessen achievement and in some cases may enhance it. Early stimulation does provide the rich soil which, with time and continued nurturance, will produce a lush, mature eroticism.

There are, of course, pitfalls in any considerable undertaking. The exercises outlined avoid the major hazards. The child who receives intense, early stimulation to one erogenous zone, like the anus, can develop such an exclusive focus that other areas and sensations are dwarfed. Medical texts describe unusual objects inserted by adults into themselves for sexual enjoyment. Coke bottles and electric light bulbs are removed from the rectums of embarrassed patients with slippery fingers. (Haft, 1973) Most cases reveal a history of early anal manipulation. Recently admitted to the pediatric ward was a seven-year-old boy with intractable constipation since infancy. His mother had treated him at home, first with suppositories, then with daily voluminous hot water enemas, until the age of six. I asked why she had ceased giving enemas then. She replied, "It was the way he looked at me when I fixed the enema bag. He was really enjoying it."

The child's personality can be affected by exaggerated anal eroticism. As intense stimulation is imposed by the powerful mother, the child begins to prefer being passive. In the boy, this predisposes to a feminine attitude through the wish to be penetrated. As the mother is the only source of stimulation, and indeed controls the enema bag, she remains of central importance. (Kestenberg, 1976) This limits the child's ability to move into other, healthier relationships, accentuating his dependency and feelings of helplessness. Other factors can predispose to passivity also. These include chronic illness and prolonged indulgence with restriction of outside interests. A reasonable balance between the active and passive modes, and a diversity of erotic foci are essential for a healthy sexual response.

Overemphasis on the genital focus can occur also, although these cases appear only in families with massive psychopathology. Rita is one such child. She was the firstborn of Jessie, a schizophrenic woman who had herself been beaten, abused, and abandoned in her early life. Jessie had been raped by her grandfather at age four and sexually molested by her mother's boyfriends. At age eighteen she conceived while following a group of Hell's Angels. The latter half of pregnancy was spent in a state mental hospital. She was discharged to a relative when Rita was two months old. This arrangement proved evanescent, and within four weeks Jessie was living in a tiny room, supporting herself and Rita through prostitution. From the time Rita was six months old, she and Jessie had oral sex together several times each day. Rita was removed from her mother's custody at age eighteen months. At three she was seen for psychiatric evaluation because of her insistent, well-calculated advances to any adult female. Rita's foster mother was afraid to lie down on a bed unless Rita was sound asleep.

An exclusive focus on one erogenous zone is easily avoided. By nature children have catholic tastes. The older infant and child only need the opportunity to develop their own, independent preferences.

In the second half of the first year the infant has almost all his eggs in one basket, and that basket is the mother, or whoever else is the primary caretaker. The baby is acutely aware of the mother's feelings, often reading her better than she reads herself. When the mother is upset the child assumes that he's to blame. For instance, Peggy's mother resents having her husband's brother living in the house because he drinks a half gallon of milk for breakfast and never cleans his room. After he leaves for class each morning she cleans with a vengeance, muttering to herself. Peggy assumes that her mother is angry with her. Her mother tends to avoid Peggy when she feels like that, but a distinctive smell heralds the need for a diaper change. "Yuk! What a MESS!" says mother. Now Peggy knows why her mother's so upset.

No parent on earth is always sunny and smiling. There'll

always be spilt milk, crumpled fenders, and checks that bounce. There's no way to prevent your child from knowing how you feel, either. However, you can protect the child's genitals from bearing the brunt of whatever happens by making them especially good instead of especially bad. A million-dollar smile accompanied by a pat with the powder to an erect penis says that the penis has value. The next time you're out of sorts, his genitals won't appear the likely culprit.

Near the end of the first year or early in the second, the child is taught the name for toes, fingers, eyes, and nose. The penis is seldom included in the lesson, and the clitoris never. Yet all important things have names, don't they? The youngster must eventually reconcile the exquisite sensations which make the genitals significant with the fact that adults don't seem to think that genitals are important at all. Maybe they shouldn't feel good. They could be dirty or bad.

A clitoris is called a clitoris—not a vagina, a "bottom" or "down there." With a bit of insight, parents can usually manage to name the penis, but fail miserably with the clitoris. Rationalizations include "It's so small she wouldn't notice it anyway," "It's too difficult to pronounce," and "Why should she need to know about that, for heaven's sake?" *Clitoris* is difficult for the toddler to pronounce. It's often contracted to "clitris" or "clis." Even so, it's far more accurate than "vagina" or "gina." Introduce the term with a smile and an adjective such as "nice," "happy," or even "yummy" to convey your enjoyment. As the clitoris is tiny, the little girl may have a geographical problem in locating the nubbin in order to name it. Given a plump tummy, this is indeed a dilemma. A mirror is helpful, or a finger may be used to identify the clitoris by touch. Whether you guide the child's finger or use your own depends upon your internal comfort. If you prefer to guide the child's finger, by all means employ the same method to identify other parts of her body, thus avoiding the message that the clitoris is untouchable or dirty.

Adults with sexual problems are generally uncomfortable with their bodies. A task assigned by many therapists is for the client to stand stark naked before a three-way mirror and her mate. She points to each bodily part and describes how it seems to her—too fat, too lumpy, so-so, or plain ridiculous. She's not allowed to skip the clitoris. Her partner completes the same task. It's rare indeed for either to say something good about the genitals. The penis is too small and the clitoris ugly or smelly. The need for treatment could have been prevented by a direct, enthusiastic approach to sex in childhood. The task which is agonizing for an adult may be ecstasy for the yearling child who struts, points, and touches with eager delight. Parents may facilitate the process with suggestions, encouragement, and obvious approval. The child's body becomes beautiful, mirrored in his parents' eyes.

During the first year of life, the erotic child has captured a profusion of pleasures. He has balanced the earlier emphasis on passive enjoyment with an active search for uniquely appropriate sensations. His parents are no longer just providers of pleasure, but distinct individuals who encourage his emotional growth.

17

SEX AND THE POTTY CHAIR

IN THE SECOND YEAR EVEN THE MOST PERMISSIVE PARENT IS faced with a grim necessity—training. The untrained five-month-old is cuddly and sweet; the untrained eighteen-month-old pulls cans off the shelf at the supermarket. When an almost-two smears food, relatives no longer smile. Bedtimes and bed rules must be observed if weary parents are to enjoy one another and a full night's rest.

Parents are between a rock and a hard place in deciding just what expectations are reasonable. Samantha's mother is an example. She's a patient, loving mommy until fourteen-month-old Samantha develops a penchant for dumping wastebaskets. Her mother places all the trash up out of reach. Samantha climbs on a chair and tumbles while grasping for a basket. She screams and displays an angry red bruise on her forehead. What should her mother do? Scold Samantha, hug her, or both?

Children this age are already aware of their parents' guilt buttons. Push a guilt button, and Christmas appears. Patrick's mother wants to leave him with a sitter so she can attend a lecture. Even though Patrick likes the sitter, he wails plaintively. Mother lugs him to class, purchasing a bag of candy to keep him quiet. Dawn is well mannered at home. In a restaurant, she bangs her water glass with the spoon. Her father removes the spoon. Dawn's lower lip grows large; she scowls and takes a deep breath. Her mother quickly lifts her from the high chair, while her father hails the waitress for a glass of milk.

A mother with an easy-to-push guilt button may become a servant to a small but imperious master. She endlessly washes, wipes, comforts, and entertains. Sometimes she reaches the end of her rope. Morris is an only child, conceived at last after a four-year, four-thousand-dollar infertility treatment. Morris developed croup and almost died at age ten months. Now Morris is chubby and active at nineteen months. His mother had been a court stenographer, but is now "only" a housewife. Her day revolves about Morris, who's regularly prammed and pampered. She forgoes the beauty parlor, because Morris pulls the magazines off the rack. His father and mother no longer attend movies because Morris squirms and whimpers. His mother has a headache by noon, but napping when Morris does seems to help. Yet by the time Morris goes to bed at night, she's once again exhausted. Invariably, she's sound asleep before the father finishes watching television.

One sunny afternoon, his mother puts Morris down for his nap and retires to her room. A soft rustle reveals that Morris is not asleep. She tiptoes in, to find Morris intently fondling his penis. "Don't *do* that! You go to sleep!" Her voice is unusually sharp as she turns Morris on his stomach. Silence, and then again, a soft rustle. The second time, Morris receives an unaccustomed swat on his rear. Why should this provoke his mother? She doesn't scold when she mops up spilled oatmeal, or when Morris sucks his thumb. The fact is that his mother hasn't gotten anything for herself for a long time. She's in a state of acute deprivation. She tries desperately to be a good mother, and a good mother gives all, all the time. And who gets it all? Morris, of course. At one time his mother did enjoy sex, but now Morris eclipses her eroticism. She's stuck in the myth of martyred motherhood. Small wonder that Morris's pleasuring is her last straw.

It would help the whole family if his mother bundled Morris off to his grandparents for a weekend so that she and his father could refuel in bed. It would be better yet if Morris could be trained to demand less and to give himself more. More erotic pleasure for Morris would allow his mother more time for herself.

All mothers aren't like Morris's. A mother at the other extreme sees all erotic pleasures as corrupting. Food is for getting vitamins and baths are for scrubbing. Two-year-old Priscilla must eat every string bean before dessert, and she mustn't hug Daddy after work because Daddy's tired. She's too heavy for her mother's lap and too old to make messes. Last year Pris could rub her clitoris, but this year she's a big girl and big girls don't do that. "You'll get your fingers dirty," "Nice girls don't do that," and "That's not what you're supposed to use that for" carry the message. Father says, "You don't want to wear it out, do you?" Again, a mother's style reflects her own sexual frustrations, not because she's overwhelmed by Pris's demands, but because of deep-seated inhibitions in which sex and dirt, gratification and corruption, are associated. She limits her own pleasures just as she limits her child's. She trains Pris as she was trained.

Most parents operate in the middle ground between these two extremes. Their approach is rational, fairly conservative, and somewhat flexible. They avoid expecting too much, but do teach the child enough to insure their own comfort. The child is no angel, but doesn't bite other children, or put his fist in the Jell-O. He protests when left with a sitter, but is soon parading before her, pulling a toy dog on a leash. Yet even these parents often convey disapproval about sex. Embraces are muted in the toddler's presence. Clothes become more important; certain topics are avoided. If the child reaches inside the mother's blouse or fondles himself, a variety of responses deflect or restrain. "Look, it's raining outside," "Your horsie is waiting to play," or "Let's find a cookie" are common. "You don't need to do that" and

'That's a no-no" are acceptably mild. Other parents prevent enjoyment by organizing the child. A plethora of activity toys surround him; a push-pull lawnmower, a miniature piano, a form board, and blocks. The day is segmented into meal time, trip time, toy time, nap time and play-with-Daddy-before-dinner time. Mother is blessed with a knack for planning, a creative imagination, and a bias against passive pleasuring.

Yet the yearling child, when given a chance, is intrigued by new erotic sensations and enthusiastically expands his repertoire. He does things because they feel great. Although he avoids activities which result in a harsh word or rough handling, he remains free of such weighty concepts as responsibility. If Aunt Figleaf is upset when he streaks naked across the living room, it's of little consequence—unless Mommy scolds or puts him to bed. The carefree toddler can still poke an inquisitive finger where it feels good. There's immense satisfaction in paddling about a puddle or dribbling peach juice off the chin.

Parents can help the child to expand his eroticism by seating him naked in a smooth-pebbled brook or a wading pool with soft rubber toys. Slides, swings, a bouncing horse, and large blow-up plastic dummies for wrestling or riding promote active stimulation. However, stick horses and sharply molded seats can painfully stifle the search for pleasure. Passive pleasuring can be enriched with back rubs, sand, sun, bubbles, a shower with Daddy, and the smell of fresh-cut grass.

Of all the tasks peculiar to the second year, potty training is the best recognized, and often the most exasperating. The potty chair brings the parent's anxieties into sharp focus. An exquisitely pleasing function must be diverted into socially acceptable channels. The child, quite rightfully, resists. Distraction won't work, and the toddler resorts to all the ploys he has tucked away to bluff parents. He's outraged, indignant, strangely dense, or utterly crushed. He remembers an urgent mission and forgets what his mother wanted anyway. He may hoard up his stool until the warm bathtub weakens his resolve. He may distract his mother and himself by pulling and patting his penis while seated on the pot.

Shame begins as a wordless concept. It stems from the toddler's perception of one part of himself as less acceptable than the rest. That part is bad, dirty, or smelly. Once established, shame is impossible to erase completely. It's the basis for the majority of problems treated in the sex clinic. Shame is the reason why it's difficult for adults to ask for certain pleasures, admit inadequacies, reveal the genitals, or even talk about sex.

The child learns to be ashamed around the time of toilet training. His parents' attitudes about control, his genitals, and the stool itself convey the concept. The anus and the genitals are somewhat distinct in a boy's mind, but a girl thinks of them as one. Thus, if diapering is a chore, the stool a stinking object to be quickly discarded, and the genitals of interest only because they must be scrubbed, the child assumes that the parent is disgusted by the whole area. The fact that adults avoid the genitals, leaving them nameless and hidden beneath clothing at all times, reinforces this theory. The child learns to keep his "privates" concealed; nothing is worse than to be "caught with your pants down."

Girls learn to be more ashamed than boys. This is related to the uncharted darkness of their anal and genital area. The clitoris is unnamed and unremarkable by any separate function such as urination. When the anus is cleansed, so are the genitals. Diapers and panties cover both, without any distinguishing aperture such as a fly. When erotic sensations arise from being wiped, rubbing against a pillow, or playing horsey, the whole area feels good. Unless the little girl has discriminated the clitoris by touch, as in the naming process, or through pleasuring, she includes her genitals in the clutter of smell, dirt, and displeasure with which she regards her stool. She confuses the odor of her stool with the smell of her genitals. As an adult, she'll continue to hide her "dirty" parts, she'll bathe daily, douche religiously, use a perfumed spray, and avoid oral sex.

Mothers communicate shame through their style of toilet training. Some commence at nine months and grimly pursue the goal of "no accidents." Others begin later, but emphasize a fast, efficient performance at the proper hour. Some solemnly examine each product for size, odor, or mushiness. Others don't train effectively and complain loudly. Some tie the toddler to the chair or punish him if he leaves. Scented sprays to cover the smell, a wrinkled nose, meticulous wiping, and hasty hand-washing accompany the effort. How can a toddler feel proud when the mother is clearly upset?

The sexually aware mother can preserve the child's enjoyment and the worth of his genitals by moderating her own reactions. She's patient, kind, and reasonably flexible. To avoid a contest of wills she delays training until the toddler's eighteen-month stubbornness wanes. She responds to the stool as an erotic product, just as she does to an erection. She smiles and comments on its pleasant characteristics. She receives the stool as warmly as she receives the child who forms it. She emphasizes the erotic rather than the hygienic component of cleansing by utilizing soft cotton, creams, and oils. She's pleased by the process. If her child is a girl, she treats the clitoris as an area distinct from the anus by naming and swabbing it separately. If her child is a boy who fondles his penis while seated on the potty chair, she observes without averting her eyes. She smiles and offers a compliment.

Anal eroticism needs to be protected too. Anal sensations intensify the adult response, providing the individual can accept and enjoy them. Tightening the muscles about the anus during coitus heightens pleasure in both sexes. Some women prefer certain positions because the penis presses back against the rectum, and in almost all positions, the woman's anus is stimulated by traction on vaginal tissues. A finger on or in the anus accentuates the climax for many men and women. Thus the mother needs to accept and convey enjoyment of the anus also. Her tissue can be soft, her touch tender, and her smile warm.

Preschool children invest their stool with character—nice, mean, powerful, angry, stubborn, and so forth. (Anthony, 1972) Children ascribe the same qualities to the stool that they assign to the anal and genital areas. It's easy to find out how a child feels by asking. Let him know that you can feel friendly toward both the producer and the product.

Occasionally a child enamored of his own products will decorate himself or a wall with astutely smeared feces. Is a parent supposed to encourage that too? Hardly. Encourage eroticism and preserve pleasure, but not at the expense of creating an "enfant terrible." This can be labeled unacceptable behavior without demeaning the stool nor the child's intrinsic worth. "Your poop is lovely, but it does *not* belong on the wall. Here, help me put it back in the pot." The production of flatus, or letting wind, can also be gently curtailed without evoking shame if the parents have first demonstrated their acceptance and enjoyment of this natural function.

Shame is transmitted to children at an age when words are less important than actions. Because of this, the sex therapy clinics must utilize actions rather than words to relieve shame. Assignments include disrobing under a bright light, swimming together nude, demonstrating methods of self-pleasuring to one another, and an exploration of each other's genitals. This last exercise includes the internal examination of the wife by her husband, in the presence of one or more therapists. An examining table with stirrups and a speculum are provided. These tasks cause the clients profound embarrassment, and the therapist must support the couple every step of the way. Once a task is complete, the clients experience tremendous relief, and increased comfort and intimacy. As shame diminishes, sex improves.

Another sexual dysfunction, performance anxiety, is rooted

in our early attempts to educate children, such as toilet training. Performance anxieties are the fears which men experience concerning erection and ejaculation. Will it get hard enough? Can I hold that erection? Can I delay orgasm long enough to satisfy my mate? Will I ejaculate? Once these anxieties intervene, the joy in sex dwindles. The production itself is so important that passive, receptive pleasuring is impossible. The child's first pressured performance is on the potty chair. Mothers who focus on the rapid production of "enough" stool at the appointed hour are emphasizing performance. "Now it's time to do your business"; "Do a good job." Goodness is equated with compliance and achievement. The child learns to please his mother by producing a proper stool. Later, he pleases his mate by producing a proper orgasm. Performance anxiety can be prevented through a relaxed attitude toward all early training including the potty chair. Slipups are expectable. In addition, parents can emphasize passive pleasures such as rocking and back rubbing, and the erotic rather than hygienic component of toilet training.

Transitional objects, like Linus's baby blanket, or a dirty teddy bear, have erotic significance, whether they be sucked, stroked, held, or used for masturbation. Like the stool, they're somehow part of the child's view of himself. They must be treated with concern. One father wrinkles his nose and pries a grubby blanket loose from Alice, an indignant two-year-old. An incident for Daddy, an insult for Alice. Her blanket is her comfort and pleasure. If it's dirty, so is Alice. If Daddy dislikes it, he objects to her also and the pleasures she receives from her blanket. Daddy needs to talk nicely to the blanket and to Alice before he gently removes the tattered remnant and dunks it in the washing machine.

A diaper is an effective deterrent to masturbation. Once it is removed, there's little to prevent the hand from rubbing, kneading, or stroking. Many a toddler seizes this opportunity to pleasure himself at bedtime or when there's little else to do. Yet Spock and others warn of "excessive masturbation" caused by anxiety or conflict. How much is too much? "Excessive masturbation" is rare, but it does occur. Most unusual at two, it remains uncommon at five. A more descriptive term would be "compulsive masturbation," which connotes the driven and singularly joyless quality of this activity. Other signs of an emotional disturbance are present, as with Peter and Faith in Chapter 10. The child is never satisfied, and uses every opportunity to continue. If restrained, he becomes more anxious and will find a way in spite of parental wrath. Parents often wonder if the child has an irritation or an itch, for the genitals are red and raw from such prolonged rubbing. Pinworms and urethritis are rarely implicated. Compulsive masturbation can be easily recognized as there's no real pleasure involved. Sex has become an expression of anxiety or anger.

Healthy masturbation doesn't interfere with activities such as taking a walk with Daddy or climbing the stairs. It accompanies relaxation, inactivity, and passive pleasuring such as taking a bath or listening while Mother reads a story. It's easily validated by a nod or a smile. Occasionally, youngsters will stroke or finger the genitals at times and in places which are inappropriate, as while riding on a train or swinging in the park. This may be viewed as similar to eating chicken with the fingers—delightful at home, but perhaps poor manners in company. A tactful "not now, wait until later," accompanied if necessary by removing the child's hand, are not amiss as long as the child already knows that you accept and enjoy his eroticism. The child who isn't certain of your feelings needs clarification and extra reassurance.

The erotic toddler is enthusiastic and spontaneous. He searches for pleasure with confidence, but already needs a few guidelines. He asks for what he wants, but doesn't expect gratification every time. His behavior is acceptable, but far from perfect. He remains proud of both his body and its products.

18

HAVE YOU GOT
WHAT I GOT?
(AGES TWO THROUGH FOUR)

THESE ARE EXCITING YEARS. CHILDREN ARE OFF THE LAP AND
into the backyard. There are tricycles to be pedaled, puppies
to be chased, and flowers to be picked. Words are now entrancing tools which can bring fairies to the bedside or persuade Mother that the beach is better than cleaning house.
The child appreciates the magic of the milk which mysteriously appears outside the door on Monday and of Daddy's
voice in the telephone receiver. He expects that adults can
make miracles, that trains can fly, and that children may be
eaten by vacuum cleaners. The world is an elixir packed with
delight, yet strangely unpredictable.

At the seashore four-year-old Trudy concocts a new sensation. She pulls open the elastic waist of her swim suit and
dumps in a pail of shells and water. Add seaweed for spice.
Five minutes later, she covers her legs with sand, wiggling
her toes to prove they still exist. She lies on her back in the
shallow water, pokes holes in the mud with a stick, and
splashes her baby brother. Her father tells Trudy to put on
a shirt to prevent sunburn. Trudy nods, but forgets her
father's instructions as she sprinkles sand on a very dead star-
fish. In a half hour Trudy investigates a dozen erotic sensa-

tions. She can't select the one she likes best or relinquish any of the other joys she's discovered. She has a repertoire of genital pleasures, none of which snares her attention for long. Trudy is a healthy, erotic four-year-old.

Passive pleasuring seems lost as the child putters and bustles about the home. The enfolding arms of a mother or the silky softness of the father's chest haven't lost their charm —but there's so little time. Often a youngster's exhilaration is terminated only by collapse in bed. The sensitive parent insists on a few quiet time-outs each day. A siesta is reserved for back scratching, holding, nuzzling, and snuggling. Naptime stories in a rocking chair balance the hectic pace of the morning hours and emphasize the importance of receiving pleasure.

Rarely, a youngster becomes all too invested in passive pleasuring, to the exclusion of swings, slides, and other children. This is most often a girl from a small family who's been protected and cuddled. Elizabeth is such a youngster. One afternoon at the park her brother, Tommy, runs to his father crying and complaining that a bad boy took his tricycle. The father tells Tommy that the other boy is exactly his size. Tommy is to demand his tricycle back. Ten minutes later, Elizabeth arrives weeping. Another little girl threw sand in her face. Her father hugs her, dries her tears, and suggests that they return home. At home, Elizabeth is a pretty child who prefers to remain inside. She loves to have her hair curled and to be read fairy tales. Elizabeth can hardly be blamed for preferring the shelter of a lap to the rigors of the playground. Her balance of pleasure has already tipped precariously away from active enjoyment. She expects to be given whatever she needs. Later in life, she may wait for her mate to provide her with a climax, and be angry when he fails to predict her erotic needs. Little girls, as well as little boys, need to be dusted off and dispatched back into the fray to settle any reasonable problem. (Baumarind, 1972)

The gravest damage occurs when a youngster is bound

closely to a sexually stimulating parent. Timothy, in Chapter 10, is such a child. Children must be free to develop erotic interests on their own, or else titillation becomes a time bomb. They need to experiment and grow outside the highly charged and necessarily frustrating relationships within the family. Children in Mangaia and other liberal cultures develop into erotically healthy adults not only because of early stimulation, but because they're free to roam the bush and experiment with one another. Children in this country need playmates and independence also.

What about the child who can't move freely beyond the family? The asthmatic must be carefully guarded against allergens and the hemophiliac against injury. An only child who lives in a rural area or a violent neighborhood is necessarily restricted. A single parent may bind a child close because of fear or loneliness. Frequent moves from place to place may prevent a youngster from establishing himself in the peer group. Such children don't need increased erotic stimulation from parents, especially after age four. The chronically ill child is a special problem. He's already amply aroused by physical ministrations such as bathing and feeding. Direct physical contact must be minimized and the child helped to be as active in his own behalf as he can. As a sick child feels more helpless, or impotent, than a well child, he needs to develop as many competencies as possible. Crafts, writing, playing an instrument, and reading are nonerotic methods of aiding potency. Parental enthusiasm about the child's independent erotic ventures is never amiss.

As the world widens, the child looks beyond his mother and father. He observes how others relate, and what effect outside events have on his parents. He makes assumptions based on scant experience and an avid imagination. With a firm belief in magic he blends the real and impossible to create theories about everyday experiences. Whenever he is anxious, fantasies sprout and flower into fantastic schemes.

One sunny afternoon in May, Aunt Figleaf pays an unexpected visit. Henrietta is stark naked, leaping about the living room after a puppy. Aunt Figleaf braces herself against the piano and informs Henrietta that she forgot to put her clothes on. "No, I didn't" is Henrietta's breezy reply as she gallops off through the dining room. Aunt Figleaf was a surgical nurse in the last world war; clean clothes and soap are to prevent disease. She delivers an unsolicited lecture to the mother about the dire consequences of germs transmitted by domestic animals. The mother listens politely because Aunt Figleaf is the father's oldest sister. Henrietta observes from the doorway, and tries to put together the puzzle. Obviously Aunt Figleaf is a powerful person and that makes her right. She certainly is upset about something—but what? Henrietta concludes that her body is bad, running after the puppy is bad, or that bodies and puppies are bad because they are dirty. She finally concludes that feeling good and being naked are dirty. Later Mother explains why Aunt Figleaf was so obsessed. Aunt Figleaf is very old, out of touch, brought up in another time. These concepts are beyond Henrietta. She extracts bits and pieces to form new theories. Aunt Figleaf is old, so is Mommy; therefore Mommy thinks it's dirty too. Aunt Figleaf has run out of touch because Henrietta is too dirty to touch. Henrietta's theories make more sense to her than her mother's reassurances. Henrietta is saved not by her mother's speech, but by her parents' wholehearted enjoyment of her nakedness.

Randy is playing in the living room one Saturday afternoon. His parents are taking a nap. Randy overhears a strange sequence of thumps and squeaks. He climbs the stairs and listens at the door. A moan? He opens the door, provoking a muffled grunt and a flurry of bedclothes. His mother's face is red, and her hair a mess. She looks frightened. His father seems angry; he tells Randy to leave. His father must have been beating his mother. Randy sits on the couch and wonders why. When his mother comes down, she hurries to the kitchen without looking at Randy. His father sits down and tells Randy that Mommy and Daddy were only wrestling. Randy has a better idea.

The little boy's first trip to the barber shop is also a frightening experience. The next expedition is still pretty scary. By the tenth time it's a delightful visit to a friendly fellow with an elevator chair. Familiarity has chased away the monster; the child is comfortable again. The youngster in Mangaia who first views coitus is every bit as terrified as Randy, but then it happens every night. Not only does his mother survive, but she appears hale and hearty each morning. Now the child begins to pay close attention. That's not his mother who groans, after all. She's hugging Daddy back. The primal scene becomes an intriguing event.

This natural desensitization process exists wherever quarters are cramped or children sleep with parents. Life goes on and the child gains perspective. In our middle-class homes, children have separate bedrooms and sex is shrouded in secrecy. Children are stuck with little knowledge and a large imagination. You may need to offer reassurance until further learning is possible. "Mommy and Daddy were hugging and kissing," is a better explanation than an aggressive concept such as wrestling. Both parents need to discuss the event with the child. Because the child commonly pictures his mother as the victim, the mother needs to hug or rub Daddy, to substantiate her pleasure openly. A detailed, specific explanation is unsuitable, simply because of the child's limited understanding and florid misinterpretations. A demonstration can succeed where words fail. Gather puppets or flexible dolls, a blanket, and an inverted box to serve as a bed. Have the puppets clasp, grunt, and roll together to your enthusiastic comments. The mother handles the girl puppet to act out her agreeable participation. Urge the child to repeat the play himself while you serve as audience. Don't be surprised if the same format is reenacted later with a neighbor child. You needn't portray genital coupling unless the child observed that aspect in the flesh.

Needless to say, the child who perceives Mommy as liking to touch and be touched by Daddy, and Daddy as listening attentively to Mommy is less likely to interpret aggressively any unusual event.

Nudity in the home has been controversial for at least fifty years. Parents fear overstimulation or promiscuity. They're ashamed to be seen naked and are embarrassed for the children also. "Here, pull your dress down before someone sees you!" "Remember to zip your pants." "I'm ashamed of you—running around like that." This rigid insistence on clothing propagates shame. In countries where nudity is common, there's nothing to hide, and no reason to assume that one part is covered because it's ugly or dirty. Unclothed children have the opportunity for much casual genital pleasuring, as in wrestling with a chum or crawling over a friendly dog.

Clothing constitutes an emotional investment. "How do I look?" is a common request for reassurance. The staid, paunchy businessman who, for the first time, ambles through the living room bare and nonchalant evokes reactions which range from anxious giggles to plans for a state hospital commitment. Children over four may be shocked or fearful when first confronted by a naked adult. The level of shame in our society is so great that any considerable change in clothing habits is as unlikely as open intercourse. We can, however, encourage children to be comfortable with their bodies by allowing them free play sessions in the nude. Mud puddles and garden hoses are ready accessories.

"Am I male or female?" is a question which must be answered by age three. How can the child learn this? Interchangeable roles, unisex clothing, and hidden genitals are confusing. It helps if he can change the baby or distinguish male from female puppies in a litter. Bathing with a child of the opposite sex provides an easy solution. Simple tub games afford both information and erotic enrichment. These include "ding dong," "push the soap," and "tie the boat." The presence of simple props and at least one boy are required.

"Ding dong" is best played by two boys. They stretch out side by side, and each peers across the water to catch sight of a surfacing penis. A quick tug is the "ding dong" for which the game is named. Boys rarely experience an erection, which would constitute a definite liability. If a girl is present, she may play also, but she has an unfair advantage. In "push the soap" an erection is profitable and girls feel hopelessly inferior. If the soap won't float, neither sex has an advantage. Girls enjoy "tie the boat," although obviously they can't play without at least one boy. Unless the player who provides the mooring happens to have an erection, the game becomes frustrating and is soon abandoned. Fortunately, neither sex can fasten an effective knot.

Toilet games enhance the pleasures of urination and defecation and provide a lesson in anatomy. In the game "show me," children perform for each other on the pot. As more of the girl's body lies hidden, she has more to reveal. Little boys are intensely interested, although no game persists for more than a few minutes at this age. In the toilet game "make a big one," the sexes are evenly matched. Needless to say, keen concentration is required. "Waterworks" is a contest which can be devastating to the little girl. Accuracy and projectile force claim victory for the male every time. Recognizing the inadequacies of her equipment, the little girl may refuse to play or retreat to her mother for solace. Boys feel incredibly proud.

Parents don't need to suggest these games. Lively children, time, and permission are all that are necessary. "After your bath, go ahead and play" is permission enough for a reasonably uninhibited child. Parents do need to monitor their reactions should they surprise the children in a sex game. An exclamation, muffled remark, or hasty retreat can provoke shame. A smile, together with a statement like "Hey, that looks like fun!" should be sufficient. Parents may then exit, so as not to interfere with the children's spontaneity.

When parents are open about their bodies, issues arise

which can be settled to the child's advantage. Chet is awe-struck at the size of his father's member. He looks at his own and is humbled. One morning, his father enters the bathroom with an erection; Chet is crestfallen. Happily, he already knows that his penis is valuable; it feels good and his mother likes it. He's reassured when his father acknowl-edges that boys have smaller organs and that when Chet is a man he will have a very large penis also.

Roger hasn't developed penis pride; he needs more than a simple statement. His father adds, "That's a very fine penis you have," or, "We're lucky to have a handsome penis that feels good too." Father can engage Roger in a simple remedi-ation to encourage penis pride. Each in turn projects a forceful stream of urine into the toilet to produce froth. His father compliments Roger and may limit the force of his own stream so that Roger's is outstanding. A capful of detergent in the bowl can add to Roger's enjoyment.

The healthy two-year-old child strips for pleasure and only gradually learns to remain clothed except at certain times. The older preschooler, commonly a girl, may strip because she's anxious. At three and a half, Nancy has a hypothesis. Like any other scientist she seeks confirmation through an extensive and varied experimental approach. She drops her pants in the park, wanders bottomless out of the public toilet, and streaks across the yard. When company is present she invariably enters naked. Averted eyes and her mother's scowl affirm her suspicions. An occasional laugh puzzles her, but the weight of evidence clearly indicates that her genitals are powerfully bad.

Nancy's hypothesis began when mother taught her to wipe from front to back and insisted that she change her under-pants when they were stained. Some months later, Nancy saw her cousin Jack urinate. Cousin Jack didn't even use toilet tissue. Nancy asked her mother why, and her mother replied, "Boys don't have to worry." Nancy thought girls were dirty because only girls needed to use toilet paper. If

Nancy had held her genitals in high esteem before these minor incidents, no such hypothesis would have been necessary.

The genitals should have been named before age two, but now the child needs to understand more about what they mean. To explain the clitoris is especially awkward for parents because it's the only organ whose sole business is sexual pleasure. Parents have used the term "vagina" because that has an explainable function: It's the passage through which babies are born. The penis is even easier because it's an unparalleled device for shooting urine in the pot. The older child may be told that it also carries semen or plants a seed. The message parents avoid at all cost is that the primary use for genitals is to feel good. Aesthetics are also omitted from the lesson. "Does it look good?" is a common concern for all of us, including the preschool child. To declare that a girl is special because she can have babies is helpful, but how will she know her clitoris is pretty? A young lady who thinks she has a dirty bottom which smells bad isn't benefited by knowing that her uterus will function well someday. Parents can say simply and directly, "That's your clitoris. It's very pretty and it gives you good feelings." The boy may be told, "This is your penis, it's handsome, it shoots urine a long way, and it feels great when you touch it."

Preschool children are less intrigued by copulating animals than they will be in a few years. The dog's genitals, however, are fascinating. Youngsters may poke or tease for curiosity and pleasure. Babies' genitals are charming also. The child may rub or kiss them to see what happens. Although terribly upsetting to parents, this is only an experiment, unless the child has been exploited sexually by adults or older peers.

Girls this age may receive their first intense arousal when licked by a friendly puppy. Loose-fitting panties and the puppy's natural bent may surprise and please. Unless the child is sorely constricted, isolated, or depressed, this is but a happy event which contributes to her overall eroticism. A catastrophe can occur if the little girl and puppy are caught enjoying one another. If the parents are disgusted or angry, or if they dispose of the dog, the child's eroticism can be severely damaged.

A good nursery school provides sex education. Other children and animals are the teachers. However, not all nursery schools are alike, and more than a few consistently frustrate the development of eroticism. Descriptive brochures rarely mention sex. The best way to find out is to visit the school and talk to the teachers. Look for shared bathroom facilities, the presence of pets such as rabbits or guinea pigs of both sexes, and tree houses, forts, or other small enclosures. The proportion of free time available and the teacher's ability to be frank and open in discussing sex are important. Ask questions such as "What do you do if Johnny pulls down Mary's panties?" and "What happens if a child watches the rabbits copulate?" If the teacher is comfortable in responding to these questions, she may be able to field your child's.

Happy Days preschool supplies its children with finger paint, sand, and clay for a free play period early in the morning. By the end of the hour the room can scarcely be recognized. Next comes a cleanup in which all participate. Then children sit in a circle while the teacher displays each child's work of art. Teachers smile and clap while the children nudge and giggle. Milk and cookies follow, and youngsters are reminded to use the toilet. For the next ten minutes there's a watch-and-wait line inside the bathroom. The teacher enters only when a child requests help, as with a zipper. A cage of hamsters sits on the playroom floor and outside is a rabbit pen.

Three blocks away is the Serendipity nursery school. Each morning children manipulate form boards, hook together alphabet letters shaped like jungle animals, and learn to use scissors. Those who master simple sums or who can tie a shoelace are pinned with a large gold star. Teachers demonstrate the proper use of toys, including a computerlike device which rewards youngsters for matching colors correctly. The children are developing "school readiness." Boys and girls are sent separately to the bathroom. The younger ones are accompanied by a teacher who supervises the use of toilet paper and the washing of hands. The child who pulls too much toilet paper off the roll is politely but firmly discouraged. Although the school has no pets, children are taken on weekly trips to farms, museums, a tomato paste factory, and a fish hatchery.

The Serendipity nursery readies children better for school while Happy Days prepares them better for bed. Overemphasis on achievement necessarily causes underemphasis on eroticism. In Serendipity, performance anxiety is hailed as a sign of success. Children graduate with a list of priorities and a series of well-practiced techniques. Youngsters who attend Happy Days learn to enjoy life while they expand their erotic interests.

At home and at preschool, the child poses questions which would confound a professor. A four-year-old queries, "Do mosquitoes got a penis?" He isn't interested in anatomical structure or the mechanics of intercourse. He has just looked closely at a mosquito for the first time and wonders if the stinger could be a penis. The three-year-old who asks her pregnant mother where babies come from wonders if the infant could drop in the toilet to be flushed away. A four-year-old who was circumcised a few months before is angry and upset when his mother prepares for the birth of a new baby. Again and again he asks why she must go to the hospital. She reassures him that he may visit her, and that Daddy will stay home from work to care for him. When she's ready to leave, he clings to her leg and sobs. He thinks his mother will be circumcised too. A three-year-old tells her mother to stop having babies. She remembers an Irish setter who gave birth to fourteen puppies, several of which eventually starved. The parent who sticks to the facts often misses the point.

There's no substitute for listening to the child and sorting through his magical confusion and illogical connections. Yet the reason why the youngster is anxious about sex and intent upon building theories is that there's precious little real information available. The deficit is not of facts, which are largely incomprehensible at this age anyway, but in feelings, attitudes, and expectations. A most effective tool for conveying these intangibles is sorely neglected—the fable or folktale. The Eastern Apache Indian tribes spin folk tales to children about the coyote who possesses an immense penis. This picturesque trickster is thwarted in his erotic exploits through his own blunders. Young and old of both sexes sit back, laugh, and joke about the human foibles of the coyote. The tale is both instructive and reassuring. Adult enthusiasm for sexual themes and approval or disapproval of various expressions of eroticism are evident. (Opler, 1975)

Parents can create their own fables or include erotic elements in stories already on the shelf. Thus the Grinch can steal a curvaceous maid along with Christmas, Dorothy may woo the Cowardly Lion, and Jack can fetch more than a pail of water. Unexpurgated myths and fairy tales may be resurrected in the service of eroticism, although only the simpler stories and fables are suitable for preschoolers. Occasionally a modern tale such as *Millicent the Monster* by Mary Lystad is distinctly erotic. Millicent threatens the boy next door while straddling a large tree limb, insults her mother, makes faces at motorists, stands on her head to reveal her underpants, and rides astride a rocking horse. The ending is moral without presenting sex or assertion as shameful or dirty. While reading aloud a story such as *Millicent*, parents can stress the pleasure in erotic activity, and embellish or enlarge upon sexual themes. Open discussion can then be encouraged.

Stories also provide a foundation in sexual responsibility.

Values such as consideration for others, honesty, and accountability are clearly conveyed. Children this age don't just listen to stories, they live stories, so that part of each tale becomes a part of the child.

The erotic preschooler has a conviction of maleness or femaleness based upon real data. He views his genitals as pretty, pleasing, and presentable. Simple sex games are enjoyed without shame. His erotic interests are now largely independent of his parents. As he expands his friendships in the future, he will find many additional opportunities.

19

OEDIPUS ACCENTUATED
(AGES FIVE THROUGH SIX)

JACQUELINE WON'T LET DADDY ALONE; SHE HUGS AND KISSES him at the slightest provocation. She climbs on his knee and rubs back and forth. Her intent is all too clear. She keeps asking Daddy to take her to the beach or to work. When he gently refuses, she complains that Mommy never lets her do anything. She petulantly declines her favorite delicacy, Mother's chocolate chip cookies. Andrew declares that he will marry Mommy when he grows up. When asked, "What about your daddy?" he seems not to hear. The child, who is now self-possessed, wishes to possess someone else. What could be more entrancing than the parent of the opposite sex? If Daddy tickles and kisses Mommy, why not Andrew? The erotic child doesn't mince words or pass up options. The statement "I want to marry Mommy" has an unmistakable genital ring even when the child has only the foggiest concept of intercourse.

Five-year-old Herman repeatedly asks his mother, "When is Daddy going to work? Is Daddy going on a trip? One evening Herman approaches his mother without pants, but with a full erection. Unabashed, he requests that she hold his penis. His mother asks why, and Herman states matter-of-factly that it feels good. His mother needs perspective, comfort, and a sense of humor not to blush, stammer, or reject Herman and his penis. Her response is momentous for Herman, who will never again be as vulnerable. He stakes his concept of himself as a sexual being on her reaction. Even the mild "That's not a nice thing to ask your mother" crushes Herman. His mother needs to sit, listen to Herman plight his troth, and thank him for the compliment. If she tells him that his penis is pleasing while she gently explains that some things are impossible, Herman can leave rebuffed but with penis pride intact.

When Herman decides that his mother is an impracticable choice, he sees his father in a new light. His father is powerful, and absolutely possesses his mother. Herman desperately wants to be like his father, and actively models himself after him. He casts lascivious glances at his reading teacher and the girl next door. If he can't have Mommy, perhaps . . . This is what Freud describes as the favorable resolution of the oedipal conflict. A little boy decides not to possess his mother but to become a man like his father. Eventually he'll find an appropriate woman. This alignment with his father militates against homosexuality and increases the child's social awareness. The oedipal period or stage is roughly between ages four and six.

During the oedipal stage, Herman needs his father more than ever. Yet he fears that his father will detect his lust for his mother. Closeness to the mother intensifies both his desire and his fright. To Herman, his father appears like a giant with a penis the size of a football. Herman feels woefully inadequate and may retreat to the garage to massage an organ which suddenly appears three sizes smaller. What Herman needs most is an empathic father. If Herman has just failed miserably in his first seduction, his father can say, "With such a good penis, the girls will really like you." After his mother rejects Herman's penis, the father can remark, "Look how big your penis is! In a few years it will be as big as mine!" When his father realizes that Herman has entertained some very nasty thoughts about him, and now is ashamed, the father comments, "I used to get awfully mad at my father too, but he understood." When Herman has learned a special skill, such as riding a bicycle, his father can endorse his potency with a statement such as, "Look at you go! A few months back that would have been impossible!" If they ride together Herman feels proud and almost as potent as his father.

If his mother is too understanding toward Herman's proposition there may be no resolution at all. Herman can feel ever on the verge of success because his mother never really says, "No." He remains afraid of his father, and uninterested in other women. His mother can say, "You have a very nice penis, but it isn't a present that a son gives his mother. Father gives me his and that's the right way. Later, you'll find a girl and give her yours."

Jacqueline's oedipal struggle is no less poignant than Herman's, although the subtle maneuvers she employs are less distressing. Jacqueline still has a problem finding her own clitoris, so she can scarcely offer it to Daddy. She offers her entire body instead. Her father perceives her as sweet and cuddly and is amused at her courtship. It's hard for Daddy to say "No" with conviction. Yet her father must set limits just as surely as the mother must with Herman. This can be done without rejecting Jacqueline's eroticism, by a statement such as "You're cute, and sexy, too, but Mommy's my sweetheart and you're my child. Someday you'll have a man to make love to you the way I make love to Mommy." The father's recognition of Jacqueline's sexuality is essential for her healthy erotic growth. Most young girls have had precious little approval from the opposite sex by the oedipal stage, whereas most boys have seen their bodies mirrored in the appreciative eyes of their mothers for years. The cues which will ease Jacqueline's entry into the adult sex role necessarily must come from her father, who represents all men. If Jacqueline knows that her father values her sexuality, then she will expect acceptance from her mate.

The mother's task is to aid Jacqueline's sense of female-ness by involving her in activities in which she can feel competent. The household tasks of cooking, making beds, and washing clothes are convenient and acceptable but only if the mother herself enjoys these pursuits. This, however, is prime time to broaden the girl's concept of femininity, ameliorating the passivity which impairs the female response. If the mother habitually gets what she wants from the father by manipulation, she and Jacqueline can practice asking directly for things. Mother and daughter can form a team in competitive sports such as kickball and volleyball. "Slap-jack" and "go fish" are excellent games to enhance assertion. As the mother openly savors victory, she gives Jacqueline permission to do the same. The mother and Jacqueline can learn to repair a bicycle tire, hang shelves, and change the oil in the family car. Whenever a skill is developed or a difficult task complete, her potency is enhanced. The father's support and approval confirm Jacqueline's worth as a com-petent female.

Clitoral recruitment is the mother's task. It's easy to com-pliment Jacqueline on the grace and symmetry of her body, but what accolade is there for a clitoris? If the mother still bathes Jacqueline, she begins by noting its beauty and pro-pensity for feeling good. Now, Jacqueline needs more than this; she needs to know how her clitoris relates to other people, and how it compares to other organs. Would Daddy like it if he saw it? Does Daddy like Mommy's clitoris? Why is it tiny compared to her brother's penis? Is his penis better because it's bigger? Why doesn't her clitoris get big and stick out? Does it get bigger later? Mother replies simply and with candor. Indeed, the clitoris is smaller and will never gain the impressive stature of the penis. It's hidden and therefore harder to stimulate. Yet it holds a very special, concentrated pleasure. The mother can comment that the nicest gifts sometimes come in the smallest packages. She can indicate that her clitoris gives her as much pleasure as

Daddy's penis gives him when they make love. Jacqueline may wonder if the clitoris is tucked away because it's bad or ugly. The mother can compare it to a wrapped and beribboned Christmas present to emphasize that objects are not hidden to conceal a lesser worth.

Jacqueline worries about her mother's anger also. If Jacqueline really does seduce her father, what would her mother say? If her father titillates her by wrestling, rubbing, or inviting her to ride on his back, Jacqueline's anxiety escalates. If the mother and father are cold toward one another, or if Daddy does indeed prefer a cuddly moppet to a harried housewife, Jacqueline's fantasy becomes frighteningly real. For Jacqueline's sake as well as their own, her parents need to enjoy each other.

Parents who derive emotional and sexual gratification from one another are unlikely to produce homosexual sons or daughters. (Rutter, 1971) Parents with a skewed or deficient relationship can predispose their offspring to homosexuality. (Marmor, 1965) An example is the mother who criticizes or resents the father, and depends upon the child for support. Or a mother may be overprotective and domineering, and married to a distant, weak father. The father may threaten or abuse the mother, driving the child closer to her and away from him.

Betty is an example of how the parents' relationship affects the child's sexuality. Betty's parents separated when she was four. Betty lives with her chronically depressed mother, who blames the family's sorry finances on the father, who "took what he wanted and left." Betty likes to play horsey with her little brother. She takes a piece of string and persuades him to put it in his mouth. She pulls this way and that, shouting commands. She threatens to switch him if he doesn't comply. Little brother doesn't like to play that game very much but Betty is an expert at persuasion. In kindergarten she attempts horsey again. Most other children refuse to play. This game isn't much fun for Betty either, but it serves a purpose. She feels in control, powerful for an instant. Betty identifies with her mother without ever having wished to possess her father. The mother is hurt, helpless, and angry at men. So is Betty.

Parents who act sexual outside the bedroom further the child's sexuality. Mutual displays of affection, including a pat on the fanny, are healthy. If the father grabs, and the mother says, "For heaven's sake, I'm cooking dinner!" the child assumes that mothers, or girls, don't like sex. An open, robust hankering for one another aids the child in establishing a positive attitude toward sex.

How can a single parent provide these essential ingredients? At times difficult, it's certainly not impossible. Simone was raised by her physicist father after her mother abandoned them both. An assortment of housekeepers cared for Simone until she was four, when she entered a day-care center. Father bestowed copious attention on his vivacious youngster. He recognized that Simone needed a mother, but remained generally distrustful of women. He and his secretary, Anne, had ventured upon a sporadic affair, but neither was prepared to make a commitment. When the father and Anne wished to make love, Simone was sent to visit Grandma. Simone only knew Anne as "that nice lady who gives me gum in Daddy's office."

When Simone was five years old she made her father pudding for his dessert and insisted on washing the bowls. Amused, the father waited until she was asleep before he rewashed the dishes. Simone made plans for her father to take her on weekend jaunts to parks and movies. Her father complied, even though the movies she chose were a dreadful bore. One Friday evening the father and Anne planned to meet. The father was preparing Simone for a visit to her grandmother's when she burst into tears and slammed the door to her room. The father's first impulse was to follow and comfort her. Instead, he sat and stared out the window. When Simone reappeared, red-eyed but silent, he informed her that she would not be going to her grandmother's because there was someone coming whom he wished her to meet. Simone was surprised and not overly pleased that the someone was that "nice lady in Daddy's office who gives me gum." In fact, Simone was unable to remember Anne's name in spite of repeated visits over the next six months. Simone refused to make pudding, or wipe a dish, and would retreat to her room after dinner in surly silence. Anne, who was now father's fiancée, accepted this spiteful Aphrodite in good grace. She proposed a shopping expedition which Simone immediately rejected. The father decided to go shopping instead, and informed Simone that she would visit Grandma's. More tears, and Simone screamed at Anne, "You aren't my mother!"

Two days before the wedding, Simone asked if she could be the flower girl. Anne and Simone went shopping for a dress. Simone became a delightful flower girl, although she was again miffed when no one invited her to the honeymoon.

Mothers who are single parents of young boys are in a difficult position also. An uncle, a Boy Scout leader, or a male teacher may serve as role model if mother lacks a steady male friend. If the mother derives major emotional satisfaction from her son she needs to monitor her own reactions closely. She may unwittingly impede his growth by seeking his approval and emotional support. Then her son feels as if he does indeed possess his mother and thus restricts himself from outside erotic pursuits. He needs to be urged, and sometimes pushed out to club meetings and sports events while his mother remains at home. Summer camp and prolonged visits to relatives are helpful.

Some young single mothers are so bound by little money and large responsibility that they appear sexually uninterested. Sandy works long and hard as a nurse's aid to support two youngsters. By the time she beds down the children and completes her nightly chores, she's too exhausted to pleasure herself, much less seek out a man. Her aseptic existence provides her little girl with a role model of grim asceticism. If Sandy's child is to view sex positively, so must Sandy.

When a young lady or gentleman comes precariously close to living out the oedipal drama of possessing the parent of the opposite sex, the best solution is to add another warm but firm parent, or the best available substitute. Then the child can once again be a child and all are more comfortable.

Children of five and six can comprehend genital coupling. Mating animals have become an intriguing sight. Big sister and her boyfriend are fascinating too. Now youngsters can be taught the mechanics of intercourse. In addition, they need to know that the penis imparts pleasure as it enters the vagina. Making love is enjoyable. Occasionally parents do it to have a baby also. If children assume, as they're often told, that intercourse is only to have babies, they expect that it hurts because of the size discrepancy between penis and vagina. Some parents put in a plug for morality with "wait for that special someone," or "it's nice, but only after marriage." Unless children have a firm erotic base, they may construe this as "sex is dirty or bad unless you're married." This adds to their shame and is difficult to alter—before or after marriage. Whether the child knows all the correct details at this age has little meaning, as long as he understands that coitus is acceptable and pleasing. Facts are grossly overrated anyway. A bright first-grader can be trained to parrot sex facts which he can't possibly comprehend. Attitudes and expectations are best learned through casual conversation or storytelling. When a parent attaches tremendous import to being right, the insistence on correctness quashes all the eroticism in the conversations and inevitably conveys anxiety.

Sex play flourishes among less inhibited kindergarten

youngsters. Graphic detail, roles, props, and complicated themes add spice to a delightful learning experience. The rule is still "do what feels good, as long as you don't get caught." Children know that sex play upsets adults. They close the bathroom door and they make good use of the treehouse. The child whose parents have encouraged eroticism soon learns from playmates that most adults frown on sex play.

Games are based upon the real experiences or observations of at least one of the participants. "Mommy and Daddy" is a classic. Two children wriggle about together, or bounce up and down on top of one another. The audience convulses with laughter, and eagerly awaits a turn. Genital coupling may not be understood by any child present, but the spirit is contagious. A variant of "Mommy and Daddy" is "big sister," a game performed by children who peeked at an opportune moment. After big sister and boyfriend have squirmed and bucked, an irate "parent" enters screaming, "You bad kids! You get out of my house!" Squeals of laughter greet this resolution. "Zoo" and "bull and cow" are played by youngsters with explicit information. The children's concept of maleness and femaleness is clearly depicted. Some "cows" act abused, others coquettishly prance away, and some compete to become bulls. Bulls may roar and charge or peevishly insist that the cow "come here right now!" Genital contact is a limited but important aspect to the play. In healthy sex play children accept as much contact as they wish, and there's never any exploitation.

A game which involves manipulation, but which rarely progresses to genital contact, is "doctor." This is easily converted to "nurse," "dentist," or "plumber"—in short, anyone who looks into anything. Commercially available doctor's sets may inspire the play but aren't usually necessary. Each orifice is examined by looking, touching, and occasionally smelling. An imaginary pill cures all ills. This game rarely proceeds smoothly, as most children are ticklish. The agile physician may need to pursue a frisky patient. If the doctor suggests a rectal temperature, the thought itself is enough to send his patient scrambling for the other side of the bed.

The middle-class child isn't into sex play just for genital stimulation. For several years, youngsters have been puzzled by parents' standoffish attitudes toward sex. Others are anxious because of the strange sounds behind a locked bedroom door, a neighbor's criticism, or their own misinterpretations. As children play at making love, the intangible becomes real and not so scary after all. For instance, Katy wobbles about on her mother's high heels, screaming at a wriggly, bouncing couple on the bed. "You dirty bobos you! I'm telling your mama!" Katy recalls feeling helpless when Aunt Figleaf lectured her. Now she's the master and those kids had better watch out.

Middle-class children rarely attempt penetration; indeed no one lies still long enough. However, middle-class youngsters who've been directly stimulated by adults, and many slum children, also, actively seek genital contact. If they've observed or participated in oral sex they may devise a game with this as the central focus. One such game is "blow the balloon," in which the initiator offers his penis like the neck of a balloon. He expands his stomach in graduated steps as his companion puffs. Of course, his partner must draw the air out also, and these "balloons" are tough to deflate. As interest in genital sex increases, the play degenerates into a simple request for pleasuring. Occasionally, an inexperienced girl will dare a boy to "kiss it." If the boy unexpectedly agrees she giggles and turns away.

Sex play is certainly healthy. Social skills are accrued and eroticism enriched. Sexual interests are focused outside the home. Both boys and girls feel potent. They're doing something new, daring, and entirely of their own design. Each other's genitals are exciting and powerful. The girl realizes that her body is desirable. The boy feels proud; his penis elicits awe. Girls and boys are clearly fascinated by one another.

In cultures where children are sexually active, sex play continues uninterrupted. Unfortunately, in our culture, there's a sharp decline in all sexual activity by the end of the oedipal phase. This is related to greater social awareness and the formation of a conscience. The child begins to live by principle rather than by "not getting caught." Many youngsters renounce in retrospect not only sex play but talking and thinking about sex. Recalling the pleasure itself is especially disturbing. Now girls are ashamed to be without a bathing-suit top, certain words are "dirty," and the bathroom door is always shut. Girls play with girls, and boys with boys. Only the erotic children blessed with sexually enthusiastic parents remain open and interested.

The degree of constriction reached at age six is a forecast of problems in the future. At this time the child's erotic foundation is complete. If there's been a paucity of sensual pleasure in infancy, a dearth of erotic relationships in the preschool years, and a high degree of shame, the child will curtail his interests and sharply limit his activity. Erotic impairment is inevitable.

Because of their sense of inadequacy and shame about the genitals, girls become more embarrassed and constricted than boys. As the years between six and puberty elapse, the majority of boys again experiment with sex, while very few girls participate. The cycle of little experience and much inhibition is initiated. Over a period of time this stunts the girl's erotic growth and accounts for the large number of married women whose erotic response is damaged or absent.

Parents who have followed the suggestions in these chapters, or who have in other ways communicated acceptance and enjoyment of sex, have promoted a solid erotic foundation. Once the child has enjoyed sex without shame throughout the preschool years his pleasure is well entrenched and open to further enrichment. He can withstand trauma, be it Aunt Figleaf, molestation, or discovery while masturbating, without forfeiting his potential for pleasure. Although he's failed in his first seduction, he remains proud of his genitals. He's ready and willing to try again.

20

HOW TO PLAY PING-PONG
WITH NO TABLE
(AGE SEVEN TO PUBERTY)

TINA'S MOTHER COMMENTS, "I GUESS I CAN BE THANKFUL because Tina's never had a problem with sex; in fact, she hasn't shown any interest at all. I didn't have to tell her not to play with herself, or to watch out for certain boys."

Whenever I hear a statement like this, I know absolutely that the child does have a problem. The theory that a child isn't sexual is simply untrue. Tina has already dealt with the issue of sex, and her erotic response has already suffered. She responds to a world of sexual silence.

In a Mexican town on Saturday night, most of the locals congregate at the central hotel. Children are seated with the family, dressed in their finest clothes. Beer flows freely and the children observe as bodies gyrate, cling, or shake on the dance floor. Father strokes Mother's bottom as they dance; the mother smiles and tickles his ear. An uncle sweeps a seven-year-old miss onto the floor, whirling her off her feet as others clap. A sheepish ten-year-old boy is persuaded to dance by an older sister who obviously delights in his improvisation. The playing field is clearly marked.

In the United States, children under the age of eighteen

or twenty-one are restricted from most establishments which serve alcoholic beverages. Yet almost every romantic setting also serves liquor. The bistro, dance hall, and R- or X-rated movies are shrouded in secrecy. Children aren't allowed to purchase certain magazines. Yet explicit accounts of rape and molestation are available in the newspaper, and suggestive scenes are daily fare on TV. This duplicity confuses as it titillates. When is sex acceptable? Where is the protocol, what are the rules? Children this age like games with clear definitions and explicit rules. This playing field is most disconcerting. The markers are hazy, the goalposts concealed, and the referee perplexed.

The relatively placid years between the oedipal stage and the turbulence of adolescence are called "latency." Freud dubbed this the sexless age, but we now know that this isn't the case (Rutter, 1971). Both sexes remain sexually attuned, although girls especially are ashamed and shy. Sex play does occur and steadily increases. By age thirteen, two thirds of the boys have been involved in sex play with girls. According to Kinsey, only fifteen percent of preadolescent girls have engaged in sex play with boys. Parents tend to underestimate the extent of this activity simply because children skillfully avoid discovery. Youngsters exude innocence, concoct plausible excuses, and conduct their affairs with discretion. They assume that adults detest sex play. Children who are caught pay an enormous price which can cripple their eroticism for life. The price is humiliation—a dramatic increase in shame, like finding your fly unzipped while delivering a lecture or realizing that you forgot to wear a slip under a transparent evening gown. An excruciating sensation that reddens the face and is impossible to forget. Most youngsters are ashamed about sex anyway, and are thus prone to humiliation. Once children are humiliated they may never again participate freely.

Elaine had always been a polite, eager-to-please, inhibited child. At age four a little boy persuaded her to watch him urinate. Tense and embarrassed throughout his performance, she bolted when he invited her to reciprocate. By age seven, she had made several friends and enjoyed playing games with them in the town park. Her group formed a "pee club," where each afternoon behind a clump of bushes they watched each other urinate. Unfortunately the bushes were on an embankment so that the yellow stream rolled out onto the cement court. A park custodian flailed through the bush to corner the girls against the fence. "You filthy kids! Don't you even know how to use a bathroom?" Thereafter Elaine avoided all sex play, the park, and even the friends she had enjoyed. She imagined that all the adults in the area were aware of her disgrace and fully expected that a letter would be sent to her mother. She had suffered a profound humiliation.

During latency, our customs continue to mark girls as having more to hide. An enclosed toilet is in the girls' bathroom at school, while the boys' has an open urinal. Showers are seldom required for girls' gym, but usually required for boys'. Girls are expected to be more circumspect about manners, language, and clothes which cover. Shirts are definitely not optional. Girls continue to feel ashamed.

Happily, some forces act to enhance the latency-age child's erotic development. Chief among these is the formation of groups. Children band together in clubs for pleasure and mutual support. Sex is often high on the agenda. The more inhibited talk about it, the less inhibited experiment. Boys' clubs may entice a girl specifically for sex play. Girls' clubs are aware of seduceable boys. As boys and girls grow older, an occasional mixed club is formed specifically to investigate sex.

The latency-age child sorely needs a sense of potency. Adults provide little direct reassurance when they assume that the child is uninterested in sex. Fortunately, other children do see each other's organs and exploits as intriguing.

Indirectly, potency is affirmed through the plethora of competencies which the child now develops. He can deliver papers, make money, wash the car, and use the telephone. He feels able to deal with almost anything—even sex. Astute parents express their pride in these achievements, and thus indirectly augment potency.

In a work-oriented family, achievement itself can become the child's central focus. Jack gallops from kite-flying to garage-cleaning to ceramics between two bites of hamburger. He disdains his mother's hug as he prepares to leave for Little League. Jack also participates in sex games at the clubhouse, but not for long. Strip poker is awfully tedious, and what do you get if you win anyway?

Parents need to balance the active with the passive in their own lives if they're to help children like Jack. Leisurely meals with time to savor the food, sunbathing, listening to music, and reading for pleasure provide gratification in which all may share. Most girls and many boys enjoy a back massage. Around the dinner table questions such as "What did you get?" and "How much did you accomplish?" need to be balanced with "How did it feel?" and "How could you really enjoy it?"

When an erotic child reaches latency, his parents can no longer protect him. If he's sexually open and responsive he may meet situations for which he's ill equipped. If he speaks frankly about sex, his group leader may be shocked. If he propositions a girl, she may tell her mother. He can be ostracized from Sunday school. All parents can do is to prepare him for some contingencies and reassure him when he meets rejection. "Chuck, Marian's parents may not like you wrestling with her. Best you ask them first." When Chuck returns home crestfallen because Marian's parents said he was too old for her, he can be helped to understand that different adults may subscribe to different values. Since his sense of potency has suffered, his father can say, "We both know that your body looks good and can feel good too. In truth, Marian may be too young for you."

Most children this age like and respect their parents. Parents are in an excellent position to guide the growth of sexual responsibility, which follows the same patterns of maturation as other values. For instance, the rule "Don't hit kid sister Eunice" generalizes into "Be considerate of those who are smaller and weaker." Contingencies are added so that it becomes acceptable for a fifth-grade boy to defend himself against a large fourth-grade girl threatening him with a rock, providing there's no teacher present to whom he can appeal. The basic components of sexual responsibility are to consider the feelings of the other person and to avoid physical, social, or emotional damage. Sex for exploitation is out, as are force and dishonesty. The partner's full and judicious consent is essential. If the parents have shown consideration for one another, and for the child, he already has a basis in sexual responsibility. Now the concept can be expanded, and contingencies added.

The number and kind of restrictions which parents impose on the child's erotic activities depend on many factors. An impulsive youngster with poor judgment may need a few more rules. Parents who are sexually confused or constricted may recommend stricter limits or greater license than advisable. Some liberal parents focus on the attainment of intimacy and present sex as a means to intensify a relationship. Religious parents may be sexually comfortable but feel that coitus is best reserved for marriage. Even strong prohibitions can be tolerated without harming the sexual response, providing the child has a solid erotic foundation. The confident, unembarrassed youngster can inhibit sexual expression without damaging his potential. He needs to retain some outlet such as masturbation, and he needs the ongoing emotional support from family and church. As with Grace in Chapter 3, a vigorous erotic response is not incompatible with early abstinence.

Kinsey clearly demonstrates that religion is no deterrent to the erotic response, although the more devoted often delay their sexual activities. Religion can aid sex by clarifying expectations and defining roles. Religion provides the playing field with luminous markers, freshly painted goalposts and a decisive referee. However, when religious principles dictate punishment for early masturbation and the cultivation of shame, the erotic response must suffer. Most religions today no longer object on principle to preschool erotic behavior—"child's play." It's a small step from acceptance to encouragement.

Enhancing eroticism may superficially be confused with exploiting children sexually. Aren't the producers of child porno encouraging eroticism? Indeed they are—together with an utter lack of responsibility and gross dehumanization. The youngster is a commodity, as is sex itself. Tenderness is an unwelcome obstacle. The child forfeits his right to the gradual evolution of sexual interests and expertise. He pays dearly for his heightened erotic response.

The child who hasn't delivered papers, cared for younger children, mowed the lawn, or done any other meaningful work will have a problem when he enters the labor force. The youngster reared by a doting, ever helpful mother is likely to strew clothes on the floor and oversleep when in college. The child who has learned to be polite and remain silent when angry will not easily express resentment to his mate. Above all, children need to learn behavior which will serve them in good stead as adults. This concept applies to sex also. Expectations for adults and children need to match as closely as possible. In Victorian times the rigid suppression of children's sexual activities made sense, as adults were also constricted. Suppression of childhood eroticism makes less and less sense today. Now women know they are sexual beings with unsurpassed abilities and appetite. They expect a climax and hope for multiple orgasms. Now men realize that the loss of semen doesn't drain or debilitate. They understand that the more they use it, the longer it lasts, and that flabby erections are likely due to trying too hard. Both men and women see sex as a major enrichment. Yet most children learn precious little about sex except what they pick up from each other. Parents show them how not to like it. Unless there are radical changes in our parenting, the next generation will be set up for frustrations and failure, just as was the last.

Latency sex play is intense. The thrust is toward physical sensations rather than gaining knowledge or mastering anxiety. The smell, sight, and touch of other naked bodies serve as a powerful aphrodisiac. In general, sex games are played by consenting, lusty youngsters who are intrigued and titillated. Complicated formats are designed to ease the shame and share the responsibility. Group enthusiasm makes sex play hard to resist.

"Quiz show" is modeled after a famous television program. Eleanor performs for a huge imaginary prize. A trip to Europe, a sports car, or a million candy bars await her. Of course, she knows it's all for fun, and the prize provides a good excuse. Her first assignment is to stand on her head and make a face. Later she removes her panties and opens her legs. For the grand prize she must act like a movie star and clasp another contestant's small but erect penis between her thighs. Eleanor is scared and incredibly excited. She's free to leave at any time, but somehow she stays until suppertime.

Variants of "spin the bottle" are still much in evidence. Flipping coins or guessing numbers may be employed if bottles are in short supply. A closet may afford privacy for the payoff, and girls are at least as aggressive as boys. Sometimes the kiss becomes a kind of coitus—an abbreviated version, as others are waiting to spin.

"Truth, dare, and consequence" is a game played by sophisticated youngsters who apply the concept of a contractual agreement. If the child fails to tell the truth or complete the dare as contracted, then the consequences are justified. Dares are within reason, at least at first.

Larry selects "truth." Marge asks him to name the girl he likes best. Although he names a pretty fifth-grader, no one believes him and so he must pay the consequences. Larry halfheartedly objects, but the majority rules. For his consequence, he takes off his pants and dashes to a certain tree and back. The tree is in full view of a highway. With considerable skill Larry dodges behind bushes while pulling his undershirt down to cover his penis. On return he grins broadly and dives for his pants. Leslie chooses a dare. She's to bring back a flower from a nearby cemetery. She reappears in a few minutes with a goldenrod. Immediately apprehended in her deception, her consequence is to demonstrate a strip show.

"Truth, dare, and consequence" is played by moral children who need a good excuse. They only agree to a nonsexual task such as "truth" or "dare." When they inevitably fail to tell the truth or complete a dare, they have a moral duty to pay the consequences. As they don't decide the consequence either, they have little responsibility in the whole matter. They're acting as good kids should, along accepted guidelines. These young innocents are of course enormously stimulated. The truths and dares are soon dispensed with and the game becomes a progression of touching, rubbing, and often genital contact. Blended with the excitement is fear, for if discovered, they must pay for their pleasure with intense humiliation. The game ends when someone imagines a footstep or when another recalls that his mother may be searching.

A latency-age boy possesses monumental erectile capacity. When ejaculation isn't present, he can progress from one orgasm to the next without needing to rest. From about age eight he notes a buildup phase which intensifies his pleasure. Ejaculations may begin as early as nine or ten. The middle-class boy may attempt vaginal penetration, but as neither he nor his partner is experienced, he usually settles for rubbing against the labia. The child of the slum may already have had coitus with multiple partners.

"Nudist party" is a liberated version of strip poker in which frolics and fantasy abound. All but the most constricted are inspired to enact themes that are common only on the analyst's couch. In one such party, a boy who unwittingly referred to his penis as a "wiener" was lavished with all the accouterments including bun, ketchup, mustard, and relish. His "wiener" remained happily erect in spite of the ketchup, which was fresh from the refrigerator. It was still too small for the bun, a fact which only increased the merriment. In another such party, girls decorated each available penis with streamers, balloons, and a painted face. In "nudist party" boys receive the lion's share of attention and a prodigious increase in penis pride.

Although most sex games are for fun, sex may occasionally be used to subjugate and degrade, as with Warren in Chapter 5. There are irresponsible children just as there are irresponsible adults. For some, sex is already a vehicle for anger and proof of power. The games employed by perverse children are simpler in design and focus upon rapid unilateral gratification.

Wrestling is a game which becomes increasingly erotic in latency. It's an excellent excuse for rubbing and holding that commonly ends in exhaustion when played by responsible children. An irresponsible child can use wrestling to coerce or debase. He chooses a smaller, weaker partner and attacks when there is little chance of rescue. The victim feels profoundly helpless, used, and abused. One such boy wrestled a weaker girl to the ground, forced a kiss, and then threw sand in her face. An eight-year-old girl subdued a smaller boy and sat on his chest while she pinned his arms with her feet. She then pulled his pants down in front of his friends and sauntered off. An irresponsible boy may use both physical and psychological pressures to violate a weaker child by forcing him to perform fellatio. The aggressor feels powerful and the victim degraded. The child who is that callous has usually led a disturbed and chaotic life. He has often been the victim of the same shoddy exploitation at the hands of an older child or adult.

"Chicken" is a sex game that is played by irresponsible children who shrewdly apply psychological pressure. Any child who refuses to cooperate is automatically a coward. The victim is a youngster with low self-esteem who doesn't feel potent enough to refuse, scream, run, or fight. "Chicken" is tasteless and unimaginative. The following example occurred in a grade-school playground.

Eddie threatened to tell the school principal that Chuck called him an "asshole." Chuck didn't remember saying that, but Eddie seemed certain. Eddie dramatized how the principal would twist Chuck's ear and expel him from school. If Chuck would join in a fun game, "chicken," then Eddie would forgive and forget. Chuck reluctantly chose to play. Eddie ordered him to scale the elm tree. Chuck couldn't even touch the bottom branch. Therefore Chuck was a "chicken" and Eddie could issue him any one command. Eddie graciously offered Chuck the choice of two alternatives. Either Chuck must persuade his five-year-old sister to play "chicken" or he must act as Eddie's servant for a whole week. Chuck would address Eddie as "master," do his homework, and suck his penis. If Chuck told his parents, Eddie would tell the principal about Chuck calling him "asshole."

Once compromised, a responsible child is subject to extortion and further indignities. Distrust, resentment, and a sense of utter helplessness result from this early form of rape. Children who feel impotent make excellent victims, unlikely to resist and easy to extort. Parents can help by boosting potency, defining healthy and unhealthy sex play, and citing some practical strategies.

As the vast majority of sex games are benign, and an important part of development, a positive approach to sex play is well warranted. Sex is a gift freely given and the child must learn how to give. Chums and classmates are the best teachers. Yet sex doesn't seem wholesome to many a harried parent attempting to raise a nice, socially acceptable offspring. Andrea's mother was a liberal until Andrea and her cousin locked the bedroom door to assure privacy. Now Andrea's mother is a Gestapo agent. Preston's cache of *Penthouse* magazines was discovered at spring housecleaning. His father gives Preston a lecture about not wasting brainpower and respecting women. Claude was caught making arrangements for a group sex party. His mother is too upset to deal with him. She sends him to his room to await his father.

Paying no attention is better than an inquisition, and a talk about the facts of life is a step in the right direction, but what's really needed is a discussion and an exchange of ideas. Yet a question like "Do you engage in sex play?" elicits a stare from an eight-year-old and a loud guffaw from her fourteen-year-old brother. All but the rare sensuous child are too ashamed to admit erotic interests or activities. A circuitous approach works best. "How old was the youngest girl ever to have a baby?" "What do other kids think of the sex education class?" "Suppose a law was passed to ban either sex or violence on television—which would be best?" "Do boys ever fall in love with each other?" "Can women have babies when they aren't married?" Such indirect, reasonable questions provoke a discussion which can then be channeled toward personal concerns. Avoid pressuring the child; if there's no response, try again another day. A pregnant woman on the block or a dog in heat presents additional opportunities.

Unfortunately, talks are usually held behind closed doors with the opposite sex excluded. This adds to the aura of shame and will make conversation about sex in mixed company difficult later. Sex seems too shameful or embarrassing to share. It's best if the whole family participates, as around the dinner table. This is the most effective preparation for the later sharing of sexual concerns with a mate.

Once comfort has developed, encourage the child to express his own opinion. Let him know that his theories are valuable, and as valid for him as yours are for you. Unless the youngster reveals a blatant misconception such as "kissing causes pregnancy," facts are unnecessary. Wait until he requests more detailed data, and then comment, "You can be proud that you had the courage to ask that." Give him the information he desires, honestly and simply. Brief, anecdotal accounts of your own erotic experiences give the child permission to talk about and perhaps to indulge in sex play. It helps greatly if both parents can indicate that they enjoy making love, and often, too. Most grade-school children refuse to believe that their parents would do something like *that*. They feel ashamed when they even think about it. They often accept sex only as a one-shot obligation to make a baby. The absence of babies is proof of parental abstinence. Children this age can comprehend and employ terms such as "intercourse," "having sex," and "making love."

If the child is not yet masturbating, he should be. Learning how is no problem, once the child is comfortable with the concept. He needs to know that you approve, and that other children and adults masturbate also. If this becomes a problem, examine your past responses closely. Gentle Spockian admonitions may have left their mark. "I'm sure you'll grow out of it," "Do what your heart knows is best," and "Well, it depends on what kind of a boy you want to be" are sophisticated put-downs. Another subtle reproach is to rationalize masturbation by relating it to a more acceptable function. Pleasuring is tolerated because Carol must learn about her body, or because Jason is nervous and needs to relax, or because the child hasn't emerged from a certain stage. Progress is equated with the relinquishment of pleasure.

Brothers and sisters may experiment with each other. Although most sibling incest doesn't cause emotional damage, there are more diverse learning experiences available in the neighborhood. If parents wish to divert the child to more acceptable outlets, this needs to be done without exacerbating shame or damaging his response. The mother usually discovers the liaison. Her first thought is to take the more responsible child aside and lay down the law. Her second thought is to protect the children by keeping their tryst secret from other children, and perhaps the father, too. Both approaches advocate secrecy and intensify shame. A family conference with all members present is the only viable solution. If either parent is judgmental or angry, a counselor may be included in the session. At first the family meeting accentuates the misery of the incestuous pair. Shock and shame rapidly subside as the children realize that specific behavior rather than dirt, blame, or badness is the issue. Their parents are neither enraged nor devastated. Quite simply, the youngsters are to redirect their sexual interests. Pleasuring with another is delightful—outside the family.

The danger of not including the whole family in a decision that affects everyone may also arise in a vacation cabin. Sleeping arrangements are condensed, and only a curtain divides the rooms. At night a child overhears his mother's hasty whisper, "Don't, Harry—this is a bad time!" or "Not now, can't you wait?" The child understands that the mother is being forced, and that the mother dislikes sex. This is more upsetting than overhearing intercourse. Parents can avoid this by renting a larger cabin, agreeing ahead of time not to make love, or by having sex and discussing it with the whole family, either before or after. One vacationing mother herded her brood out toward the playground after lunch. "Dad and I want time to make love—we'll open the front door when we're through." The children, of course, peeked through the window.

At the conclusion of latency, the erotic child has gained

expertise, a sense of fairness, and consideration for his partner. He has avoided humiliation and remains both proud and potent. He feels that his parents understand and approve of his erotic activities. Sex is a comfortable topic for the whole family.

21

THE ENDLESS TRANSITION

> For vulnerable teenagers, sexual gratification is
> really a peripheral issue to the sexual event.
>
> —M. W. COHEN and F. B. FRIEDMAN

EROTICISM ISN'T THE CENTRAL ISSUE FOR TODAY'S ADOLESCENT.
Sex is twisted and stretched to serve other concerns. It's used
to establish individuality, to express anger, to relate to
classmates, and even to commit a kind of social suicide. Erotic
activity makes a fine weapon for an angry adolescent in a
sexually anxious or repressive family.

Adolescence is the time between puberty and the assumption of the adult role, whether by marriage or through entering the job force. It begins with an incredible expansion—in
growth, in ability to reason, and in libido. Hormone production increases enormously, yielding sexual and aggressive
urges which frighten "nice" youngsters. Girls are ashamed as
breasts enlarge and pubic hair sprouts. It's as if their bodies
proclaim the feelings they've tried to hide. Even the mother
is banished from the bedroom when the daughter decides to
undress. Boys are intrigued by the relative size of each other's
genitals and are forever making unfavorable comparisons.

Broader issues eclipse eroticism. The child must pull away
from parents and their principles to establish a separate self.

As this process begins, the youth sees the parents' values as priggish and arbitrary. The girl who kept her room reasonably neat is angry when her mother complains that it's now a total mess. The boy who was polite and responsible is moody and unpredictable. As awful as adolescence may be for parents, it holds a high potential for emotional growth and remodeling. As adolescents form a separate self, shame may lessen, allowing the sexual response to expand.

If parents are open and enthusiastic about erotic matters, their offspring are unlikely to use sex as a weapon to assert their independence. There's no point in provoking if no one gets upset anyway. In effect, this frees sex from issues which impede its development. Battles are fought in other areas while erotic growth advances in its own inimitable fashion.

A hundred years ago, the average age of becoming an adult was fourteen, whether by marriage or by entering the work force. Now a thirty-year-old graduate student may still be an "adolescent," dependent upon his parents. Adolescence not only *seems* interminable—it *is*. Without strong religious and family supports, it becomes less and less reasonable to expect young people to refrain from coitus. By the time independence is finally achieved, the prime period for sexual learning has been left far behind. The individual is less malleable and has fewer opportunities to extend his boundaries. Dysfunctions are already well entrenched.

Janet was a seventeen-year-old girl who believed her mother's warning that "boys don't respect girls who let them do anything." Janet had been courted by only a few compliant chaps who were also family friends. Activities were well defined in advance. In the back seat Janet was so worried about what might happen next that she felt little excitement. She allowed certain caresses because "he was nice enough to take me out." She was unaware of any erotic needs of her own. When Janet turned twenty-four, her eighteen-year-old sister was married. Three months later, Janet was engaged. She attempted coitus but experienced such sharp pain that she consulted a gynecologist. He informed her that she had tight muscles and needed to relax. Janet tried desperately to relax with no success. After a year of unconsummated marriage, Janet and her husband, Larry, consulted a sex therapist, who instructed Larry to gradually insert one lubricated finger and eventually two. Bit by bit, Janet became accustomed to this strange sensation. As she relaxed, she felt pleasure for the first time. Janet was desensitized with difficulty at age twenty-five, a process that would have been simpler at age fifteen.

Parents of teenagers are in a quandary. Nothing they do seems to turn out right anyway. Many become stricter because there's so much more to restrict. One parent comments, "To hell with sex education—I just hope I can get through without strangling her!" Somehow it's worse for girls to be sexually active than for boys. Parents caution, "Watch out for those smooth-talking jocks," "Boys are just out for you-know-what," "Guys have to learn to respect girls," and "Boys are more interested in sex than girls are." As parents become more upset, the comments get stronger. "Girls who play around get venereal disease," "Boys don't respect girls who give in," and "You don't want to do something that leaves you feeling dirty, do you?" are not uncommon. Further efforts range from a heart-to-heart talk to virtual imprisonment in the house. The battlefield is now well marked. Parents are less concerned about the boys. A few wild oats are expected. However, parents may worry that the youth will forget his studies once he finds out about sex or that some loose woman will trick him into a hasty marriage via pregnancy. Sex is viewed as many things other than normal and healthy.

As the child becomes an unmistakably sexual being, the parents' own problems are brought into focus. Many a cold war becomes hot, and many an aging mentor acts like an idiot. For instance, the mother gives Virginia permission to date at age fourteen; the father accuses the mother of turning Virginia into a whore. As Sam and his father watch a passing Lolita, the father gives pointers on how to score and vividly describes the girl undressed. Melissa's exploits intrigue her mother, who insists on all the details. She emphatically states that Melissa wouldn't *really* do anything like that. Melissa's father listens in stony silence. Bernie's father risks a coronary in a frenzied effort to beat his son at tennis. Bernie's girlfriend is watching. Amy's mother is upset to learn that fifteen-year-old Amy is pregnant. Shortly thereafter, her mother also conceives and delivers within a week of Amy. Tanya's mother waits up anxiously each night for Tanya to return home. Her sleeping pattern is altered, so that she no longer has sex with Tanya's father. These problem parents bias the youth's eroticism through their own quirks and quandaries. To benefit the adolescent, they must first help themselves.

Sexual development in adolescence is divided into three stages. Early adolescence is the most turbulent. It starts with a growth spurt and the first signs of puberty. Girls begin as soon as ten, and boys two or three years later. Middle adolescence commences at about age fourteen in girls and a year or so later with boys. Late adolescence occurs at about seventeen and extends for an indefinite period.

Throughout the three stages, there are predictable changes in the kind and quality of relationships and the degree of responsibility and intimacy achieved. The initial turbulence decreases and social competencies increase. The sexual response progresses and matures through the three stages in concert with other changes. This is certainly true of the erotic child. However, the maturation of the erotic response depends upon the degree of shame, parental attitudes, and the absence of major conflicts.

EARLY ADOLESCENCE

Yesterday a happy and cooperative child, April is now a moody stranger. She resents drying dishes, eats everything in sight, and flagrantly misinterprets her mother's kindness. She spurns family outings and churlishly slams the door to her room. Her parents wonder what on earth has happened.

Beneath the facade of carefree bravado or callous indifference, the early adolescent is still notably dependent on his family. It's difficult to break away from bonds that mean so much. The youth who has the closest ties often presents as much difficulty or "turmoil" as the angry, ambivalent adolescent. Yet in order to achieve maturity he must establish a distinct self. This means a separate sexual self also. If the mother has been unwittingly seductive, severe behavior problems may arise, because the task of separation is doubly difficult.

Edith and Candy have been good friends since the fifth grade. At least one night out of each weekend is spent together. They giggle and whisper until two A.M. Candy has a crush on her math teacher and Edith is in love with Stevie Wonder. Edith is well aware that her parents won't let her date until she's sixteen; Candy knows that her math teacher is married. As they spin fantasies about a beloved, each is intensely aroused. Soon Edith is playacting; she's Candy's math teacher and this is their wedding night.

Edith and Candy are rehearsing for the future. Boys are still shorter, less developed, and kind of scary. But Edith and Candy are comfortable with one another. They understand each other's bodies and can knowingly create special sensations. Yet what do they dream about? Men.

Boys relate to boys more easily also. Two boys can travel together without being teased by a kid sister or questioned by parents. The approach is smooth and there's never any concern about who should pay the bill. Whether these young men will remain exclusively homosexual has been determined many years before.

If sex were condoned from childhood, early adolescent homosexual liaisons would be less important. Children's sex play would follow an uninterrupted continuum, gradually evolving into heterosexual coitus. In our culture, early adolescent homosexual liaisons involving sex play are frequent, normal and necessary. They pave the way to later heterosexual unions. Especially for girls, they provide remediation for the abysmal lack of earlier sex experience. Shame is ameliorated while sensate foci are developed. Girls learn what feels good and how to ask for it.

Parents who fear homosexuality will derive scant comfort from these statements. Yet simple observation can determine if the child is basically heterosexual. Let's look at Kent, age fourteen. His mother has just overheard Kent and his best friend, John, masturbating one another in the bedroom. Mother's alarmed, but pauses to evaluate the situation. Kent likes doing things best with Dad. He plays baseball with his younger bother, although lately he's been irritated when his little brother tags along. He has a picture of Farrah Fawcett on his wall, and he and John have several tattered issues of *Stag* stashed in the garage. Kent is eager to attend school parties, although he spends most of his time gathering courage rather than dancing. Fortunately for Kent, his mother decides against a confrontation.

Beneath the adolescent's seeming nonchalance lies vulnerability. A pimple becomes a disaster and a slip of the tongue a calamity. In a moment he can slide from a pinnacle of power to the depths of inadequacy. His perceptions waver with the tide of self-esteem. One moment his penis seems like a fine Havana cigar, and the next, like a damp cigarillo. Actions are confusing too. A girl who posts a "Keep Out" sign in red on the bathroom door so no one will see her undress sneaks off to school in a halter top in the dead of winter. Another day she goes braless beneath her brother's tee shirt, carefully hiding her nubbins under an unnecessary armful of books. She's searching for her sexual self by trying on roles and testing the reactions of others.

Although the adolescent's sense of potency can be enhanced by favorable comments about his skills or appearance, comments about the penis, the breasts, or sexual prowess are best shelved for the time being. The early adolescent is as prone to misconstrue as the five-year-old. A simple statement such as "Your penis is really growing" may be interpreted as an incestuous advance, an implication that the penis is too small, or a push toward intercourse. In the middle class, most early adolescents are totally unprepared for heterosexual coitus. Pointed comments about sex can frighten the youth and make him feel even *more* inadequate than he felt initially. It's also important that parents not undermine the young person's associates no matter how scruffy or obnoxious they seem. This can be accomplished without abandoning values and limits. Amy's friends use terms like "fuck" and "shit" with abandon. Mother states, "I don't like those terms and I don't want them used in my house." If Amy returns later waving the banner of free speech, her mother maintains her original principles while she reassures Amy of her intrinsic worth.

The knack of successful parenting is neither to over- nor underreact to adolescent behavior. Calmness, persistence, and patience count. Stick to your principles without shouting or striking, and without giving up, either. Reasonable rules need to be reasonably enforced. Discussions about acceptable behavior allow the youth to maintain a modicum of potency. He needs to make as many of his own decisions as possible. Regardless of how irresponsible the adolescent seems, underneath he retains the values learned in childhood. Continue to teach him by remaining strong and by caring for one another.

An early adolescent can appear much sicker than he actually is. He may have limped along with various problems for years and yet have blended in with his classmates. The surge of sexual and aggressive feelings may bring his shortcomings into sharp relief.

Fourteen-year-old Chester was such a youth. Although an excellent student, Chester was shy and had never made friends or indulged in sex play. He lived alone with his divorced mother, a responsible but mousy woman. One evening Chester left his door wide open while he lay masturbating on his bed. The apartment was tiny and Chester's room centrally located, so that his mother couldn't avoid noticing. She tried her best to pay no attention, but she was too nervous to concentrate on anything else. Finally she asked him to shut the door. Chester acted as if he didn't hear, and continued to masturbate. He repeated this performance several times each week. After a month, his mother was a nervous wreck. She consulted a male psychologist who suggested that Chester enter treatment.

The psychologist learned that Chester fully appreciated his mother's upset. Her bewilderment made him feel strong. When his therapist asked if he wanted to make love with his mother, Chester was shocked and angry. In fact, he couldn't imagine sex with anyone. Chester was dealing with the same issues as a four-year-old who plays "waterworks" or "show me." He was assessing the value of his penis. It had to be powerful if it could upset his mother like that. As Chester continued in treatment he derived a firmer sense of maleness through his therapist. He joined the ecology club, worked on the school newspaper, and gradually made friends.

MIDDLE ADOLESCENCE

Middle adolescence begins as the youth reaches some emotional equilibrium within the family and can focus greater attention outside the home. Sports events, camping trips, and parties enable him to meet the opposite sex and gradually overcome shyness. Friends provide the encouragement and soon liaisons can be made. Formal dates seem uncomfortable while casual encounters are not. The middle adolescent of fourteen to sixteen is in a unique position, admirably suited to erotic growth. Boys can have frequent ejaculations with little respite. Both sexes have boundless energy and multiple opportunities. Pleasuring can easily be enriched when the level of shame permits. Tomorrow seems far away. Concepts such as security and commitment are not yet relevant. Sex can truly be a gift freely given, with no strings attached. Although few middle-class adolescents are comfortable enough to take full advantage, this is the second golden age of sexual growth. A host of secluded nooks await an evening's tryst. There's time to concentrate and the ingenuity to create new combinations of old sensations. Flesh is warm and soft, and smells as good as mother did. The delights of infancy can be realized once more through taste, touch, and smell. Without the yoke of solemn promises and "forever" expectations, learning proceeds swiftly.

Middle adolescence is the last whistle-stop before issues such as constancy and commitment appear. Contacts are indeed more superficial and selfish than in adulthood. They are not as scary as when there's a real commitment. The boy or girl doesn't risk as much, is less vulnerable and freer to experiment. For instance, it's easier to learn how to argue constructively when the sky isn't about to fall on your head. Through multiple couplings, the youth appreciates what sort of partner is comfortable and what kind of relationship fulfilling. He develops social and erotic competencies as well as a sense of self. (Bryt, 1976) The adolescent who takes entire advantage of this period is unlikely ever to need a sex clinic.

The sexually anxious adolescent isn't free to experiment. A host of contingencies and hazy concerns about reputation and respect prevent him from forming multiple contacts. He's restricted to quasi-meaningful relationships that limit learning. Sixty years ago sex was acceptable only in marriage; thirty years ago an engagement provided tacit permission. Now "going steady," a watered-down commitment, is the standard rationale. Yet, any commitment is an obligation that blocks the acquisition of knowledge and experience. The "nice" middle-class adolescent is a good prospect for sex therapy in the future.

As the mistrust and overreactions of early adolescence fade, parents may again deal directly but gently with erotic issues. Although the enthusiastic youth needs no urging, his timid cousin may benefit from a brief comment: "The time when you feel comfortable is the time to begin" or "These are the years to learn all you can, so you know what's right for you" or "This is the season to explore; you can settle with just one later." The message is that sex is wholesome and that the adolescent is capable of making independent decisions. Be careful not to urge the youth who's far from ready, as this can only increase his helplessness.

Pragmatic issues must be discussed. Venereal disease and contraception head the list. Deliver useful information matter-of-factly. Types of contraception, their efficacy, and where to find them are important matters. If venereal disease has been understood as a malady that rots the sex organs, then correction, reassurance, and information about treatment are indicated. *Sex and Birth Control* by Lieberman and Peck and *Youth and Sex: Pleasure and Responsibility* by Gordon Jensen are useful supplements.

A boy needs to know that ejaculation, however frequent, is normal and doesn't debilitate or cause mental problems. Those archaic concepts are still alive in the locker room. Ejaculations may be presented as an intensely pleasurable gift, infinitely renewable. The youth needs to know that quality is more important than quantity of orgasms. He could have inferred the opposite from seeing an erotic movie where the hero fires away like a twenty-gauge shotgun into a dozen damsels. He needs to know that no man is always capable of an erection and that erections may wilt as anxiety mounts.

The girl without a firm erotic foundation has at best a fragile response. Shyness, shame, and formless apprehensions are enough to sabotage pleasure. She needs to know that an insufficient response isn't unusual, but that it does constitute a problem, for which there is definite remediation. She may need to develop her erotic response through masturbation. Only the most comfortable of mothers can impart this information without anxiety. Fortunately, instructions are available in books such as *Becoming Orgasmic* by Heiman, Lo-Piccolo, and LoPiccolo. The mother can purchase the book and offer to discuss it or to provide lubricants and mechanical devices if the girl wishes. If there's no lock on her bedroom door, get one.

For centuries, a girl's power has been to withhold favors while continuing to attract. If she yielded to temptation, her value in the flesh market would plummet. Passivity, stubborn refusal, and absence of lust contributed to her image as a "nice girl." These concepts are still very much in evidence. A girl needs to know that she possesses as strong a sex drive as a boy and that her satisfaction is equally important. She needs to assume the ultimate responsibility for her own arousal, which means finding out what pleases, and asking for it. She needs to understand that nice girls do talk about and can initiate sex, and that fantasies are both enjoyable and useful. You can support her right to decide what she wants and when she wants it. She needs practice in saying "yes," just as she needs practice in saying "no." For the latter, she should be aware that boys aren't harmed by not being able to ejaculate.

Most parents paddle upstream in order to accept these concepts which contradict so many traditional values. The occasional comfortable parent is less upset by the intense but evanescent liaisons of the adolescent. It's as if the youth has been granted a season's pass to an amusement park. A pass is a very special award; the season is brief and will soon be over. This is a special dispensation in the service of knowledge. His mistakes are allowed and his sexuality accepted.

Acknowledgment of sexual behavior in adolescence doesn't mean that responsibility is dead. The responsible child retains some consideration for the partner throughout adolescence and returns to full accountability as an adult. In order to learn efficiently the youth must be self-serving in his relationships. Free and fickle, he gathers the nectar and avoids the consequences. Oddly enough, this inconstancy becomes the basis for later commitment. The experience gained through multiple relationships enables him to know who he is and what he stands for. He emerges with a coherent self. For the first time he has something real to commit to another. (Erickson, 1968)

Erotic movies are ostensibly forbidden and therefore more intriguing to the teenager. Entrance is easy, and the experience entertaining to say the least. Although some material can be upsetting, the eroticism rarely is. These movies are less attractive to girls than to boys simply because they're made by men, for men. Men are portrayed as infinitely potent and women as receptacles entranced by the proficiency of the penis. Heroines savor the taste of semen as they would a cheese fondue. When adolescents attend pornographic films, the result is an immediate arousal. Intercourse or masturbation is more likely in the hours which follow. Perverse scenes aren't imitated unless the tendency already exists. Repeated exposure to erotic movies dulls the appetite and lessens the effect.

Pornographic films are also an adjunct to sex therapy. Inhibited adults view scenes of masturbation, homosexuality, and coitus in technicolor. This facilitates communication and aids in the exploration and acceptance of erotic needs. Fantasies inspired by the films may be used to promote or intensify an orgasm. Adolescents who sneak into adult movies partake of the same process.

Males have traditionally been easily aroused at the sight of a nude woman. Yet only a minority of women are excited when they see a naked man. A number report mild revulsion on viewing a penis, which reflects a longstanding inhibition of their sexual response. However, women are changing. Dr. Seymour Fisher states that: ". . . not only are many women highly aroused by visual stimuli (some women reach a level of arousal that few men attain) but also that the main differences between the two sexes are small and almost nonexistent in the most recent samples studied. . . . I would suggest that the small differences which now are detected will disappear as soon as it is more socially acceptable for women to be 'turned on' by visual sexual stimuli, and also to admit it freely."

Still, many girls touch a penis as if they could catch poison ivy. Even at the varsity swim meet they avoid glancing below the waist. The less constricted describe the penis as small or large but never as impressive or handsome. Yet the girl who can delight in the sight of the male organ will enjoy her mate's, thus adding to the pleasure of both. How can a parent facilitate this? A mother can aid the adolescent girl by demonstrating active appreciation. She can glowingly appraise a graceful Greek youth, sans fig leaf, at the museum of ancient history, or an eloquent etching from *The Joy of Sex*. The purchase of a painting, certain posters, or even a subscription to *Playgirl* can carry the message.

When the second golden age is over, the erotic adolescent has the knowledge and the expertise. He's comfortable with his own sexuality. He knows what he is, what he wants, and in good measure how to get it.

LATE ADOLESCENCE

As the late teen contemplates further school or vocational aspirations, the character of his relationships changes. Trial and error is no longer necessary. The hectic pace slows and values are reassessed. Mutual interests, satisfaction, and cooperation come to mean more than the partner's worth in the flesh market. Selfishness yields to loyalty and sharing. These changes are possible only because the youth's identity has crystallized. His path is clear and his goals defined. A commitment can be made and intimacy is at hand.

Very few adolescents make a lasting commitment at the age of seventeen, and intimacy is a process that evolves at least into the early twenties. A number never progress beyond mid-adolescence, but continue to form self-serving liaisons as adults. They choose a partner for status, as a window display, or for security. Through marriage they may gain a servant, a bank account, or a mechanical aid to masturbation.

To the sexually astute older adolescent, parents are no longer the givers of allowance or takers of privileges. They're separate people with distinct erotic needs and interests. The mature erotic adolescent expects parents to be sexually active, and encourages their eroticism.

EPILOGUE

THE SEXUAL RESPONSE IS LEARNED, JUST LIKE ANY OTHER BE-havior. It follows a natural progression throughout development. Certain aspects are appreciated at certain ages in consonance with overall physical and emotional growth. If the time for learning passes without the opportunity, the sexual response must suffer. Teaching an erotic response to a dysfunctional adult is like teaching a deaf person to sing—certainly possible, but the results may be disappointing.

The earliest experiences are clearly the most significant. Even "mature" orgasmic pleasure depends upon the freedom to be childish in bed. At the sex clinic, remedial exercises for sexual dysfunctions are analogous to children's sex play. Only through a journey back to childhood are inhibitions softened and shame alleviated. If prevention is to occur, it must occur at home—in the cradle, at the knee, and on the hobbyhorse.

We no longer preach to children about moral pollution and the evils of self-abuse. Instead we offer inattention, avoidance, and mild dissuasion. We assume that sex, like Topsy, "just grows." It's high time to rethink and redirect our efforts toward providing the child with a firm erotic foundation. We need to augment penis pride, clitoral consciousness, and a sense of potency. We can accomplish this through considered encouragement and the open acceptance of children as sexual beings. Once a firm erotic foundation is laid, sexual expression can be gently shaped through principles of honesty and responsibility. Our commitment to the future is to the children of today.

BIBLIOGRAPHY

Abernethy, V., B. Robbins, G. L. Abernethy, et al. "Identification of Women at Risk for Unwanted Pregnancy," *American Journal of Psychiatry*, Vol. 132, October, 1975.

Adams, R. N. *The American Family*. Chicago: Markham, 1971.

Anthony, E. J. "An Experimental Approach to the Psychopathology of Childhood Encopresis," *Childhood Psychopathology*, edited by S. I. Harrison and J. F. McDermott. New York: International Universities Press, 1972.

Baker, B. *On the Curability of Certain Forms of Insanity, Epilepsy, Catalepsy and Hysteria in Females*. London: Harwicke, 1866.

Baker, I. G. "The Rising Furor Over Sex Education," *Family Coordinator*, 3:210, 1969.

Bakwin, H. "Erotic Feelings in Infants and Young Children," *Medical Aspects of Human Sexuality*, Vol. 8, No. 10, 1974.

Barclay, A. M., and R. N. Haber. "The Relation of Aggression to Sexual Motivation," *Journal of Personality*, 33:462, 1965.

Baumarind, D. "From Each According to Her Ability," *School Review*, Vol. 80, No. 2, 1972.

Belmont, H. "Psychodynamics of Development," Hahnemann Medical College Seminars, March, 1975.

Bender, L., and A. Blau. "Reaction of Children to Sexual Relations With Adults," *American Journal of Psychiatry*, 7:500, 1937.

Bender, L., and A. Grugett. "A Follow-up Report on Children Who Had a Typical Sexual Experience," *American Journal of Orthopsychiatry*, 22:825, 1952.

Benedict, R. "Continuities and Discontinuities in Cultural Conditioning," in *Childhood in Contemporary Cultures*, edited by M. Mead and M. Wolfenstein. Chicago: University of Chicago Press, 1955.

Benedict, R. *Patterns of Culture*. Boston: Houghton Mifflin, 1934.

Benjamin, J. D. "The Innate and the Experiential," *Childhood Psychopathology*, edited by S. I. Harrison and J. F. McDermott. New York: International Universities Press, 1972.

Bennett, S. L. "Infant-Caretaker Interactions," *Journal of the American Academy of Child Psychiatry*, 10:321, 1971.

Bibring, G. L., et al. "A Study of the Psychological Processes in Pregnancy and of the Earliest Mother-Child Relationship," *Psychoanalytic Study of the Child*, 16:9, 1961.

Bidgood, R. E. "The Effects of Sex Education: A Summary of the Literature," *SIECUS Report*, 1:11, 1973.

Bowlby, J. *Attachment and Loss*, Vol. I. New York: Basic Books, 1969.

———. *Attachment and Loss*, Vol. II. New York: Basic Books, 1973.

Branfenbenner, V. *American Families, Trends and Pressures*. Washington, D. C.: U. S. Government Printing Office, 1974.

Brazelton, T. B., B. Koslowski, and M. Main. "Origins of Reciprocity: Mother and Infant Interactions," *Origins of Behavior*, Vol. I, edited by M. Lewis and L. Rosenblum. New York: Wiley, 1973.

Brecher, E. "History of Human Sex Research," *Comprehensive Textbook of Psychiatry*, second edition, edited by A. Freedman and H. Kaplan. Baltimore: Williams & Wilkins, 1975.

Brecher, E. M. "Krafft-Ebing *vs.* Havelock Ellis: Contrasting Attitudes in Two Pioneering Students of Sexual Behavior," *Medical Aspects of Human Sexuality*, Vol. 7, No. 7, 1973.

Brecher, E. *The Sex Researchers.* Boston: Little, Brown and Company, 1969.

Briggs, D. *Your Child's Self Esteem.* New York: Doubleday and Company, 1970.

Bruch, H. *Eating Disorders.* New York: Basic Books, 1973.

Bryt, A. "Adolescent Sex Crises," *Medical Aspects of Human Sexuality,* Vol. 10, No. 10, 1976.

Calderone, M. "Address to the International Congress of Sexology," Montreal, Canada, 1976.

Calderone, M. "Education for Sexuality," *Comprehensive Textbook of Psychiatry,* second edition, edited by A. Freedman and H. Kaplan. Baltimore: Williams & Wilkins, 1975.

Caldwell, B. "The Effects of Infant Care," *Review of Child Development Research,* edited by M. Hoffman and L. Hoffman. New York: Russell Sage Foundation, 1964.

Campbell, J. *The Mask of God: Primitive Mythology.* New York: Viking Press, 1969.

Chess, S., M. Rutter, and H. G. Birch. "Interaction of Temperament and Environment in the Production of Behavioral Disturbances in Children," *American Journal of Psychiatry,* 120: 142, 1963.

Chess, S., A. Thomas, and H. Birch. *Your Child is a Person.* New York: Viking Press, 1972.

Chilman, S. "Child Rearing and Family Relationship Patterns of the Very Poor," *Welfare in Review,* Vol. 3, 1965.

Church, J. *Understanding Your Child From Birth to Three.* New York: Random House, 1973.

Cohen, M. W., and F. B. Friedman. "Non-sexual Motivation of Adolescent Sexual Behavior," *Medical Aspects of Human Sexuality,* Vol. 9, No. 9, 1975.

Collias, N. E. "The Analysis of Socialization in Sheep and Goats," *Ecology,* Vol. 37, No. 2, 1956.

Comfort, A. *The Joy of Sex.* New York: Crown Publishers, 1972.

The Commission on Obscenity and Pornography. *The Report of* the *Commission on Obscenity and Pornography*. Washington, D.C.: U.S. Government Printing Office, 1970.

Committee on Adolescence, G.A.P.: *Normal Adolescence*. New York: Scribner, 1968.

Conn, J. H., and L. Kanner. "Children's Awareness of Sex Differences," *Journal of Child Psychiatry*, Vol. I, 1947.

Cuber, J. F. "Sex and the Upper Middle Class," *Medical Aspects of Human Sexuality*, Vol. 8, No. 7, 1974.

Cuber, J. F., and T. V. Harroff. *The Significant American: A Study of Sexual Behavior Among the Affluent*. New York: Appleton, 1965.

Davids, A., R. H. Holden, and G. B. Gray. "Maternal Anxiety During Pregnancy and Adequacy of Mother and Child Adjustment Eight Months Following Birth," *Child Development*, 24:993, 1963.

De Beauvoir, Simone. *The Coming of Age*. New York: Putnam, 1972.

Dodson, F. *How to Parent*. New York: New American Library, Signet Books, 1971.

Drysdale, C. *Elements of Social Science*. London: E. Pruelove, 1854.

Ellis, H. *Studies in the Psychology of Sex*. 2 vols. New York: Random House, 1936.

———. *My Life*. Boston: Houghton Mifflin, 1939.

Erhardt, A. A., and J. Money. "Progestin Induced Hermaphroditism: I.Q. and Psychosexual Identity in a Study of Ten Girls," *Journal of Sex Research*, 3:83, 1967.

Erickson, E. H. *Childhood and Society*. New York: W. W. Norton, 1950.

———. "Identity and the Life Cycle," *Psychological Issues*, Vol. I, No. 1. New York: International Universities Press, 1959.

———. *Identity, Youth and Crisis*, New York: Norton, 1968.

Feinstein, S., P. Giovacchini, and A. Miller. *Adolescent Psychia-*

try, Vol. I, Developmental and Clinical Studies. New York: Basic Books, 1971.

Fenichel, O. *Psychoanalytic Theory of Neurosis.* New York: W. W. Norton, 1945.

Ferreira, A. J. "The Pregnant Woman's Emotional Attitude and its Reflection on the Newborn," *American Journal of Orthopsychiatry,* 30:553, 1960.

Fiasche, A. "Sex in the Slums," *Medical Aspects of Human Sexuality,* Vol. 17, No. 9, 1973.

Finch, S. "The Effects of Adult Sexual Seduction on Children," *Medical Aspects of Human Sexuality,* Vol. 7, No. 3, 1973.

Fink, P. "Understanding Male and Female Eroticism," *Medical Aspects of Human Sexuality,* Vol. 8, No. 5, 1974.

Fisher, S. "Commentary on Sexual Phantasies in Men and Women," *Medical Aspects of Human Sexuality,* Vol. 7, No. 5, 1973.

Fisher, S. "Female Orgasm," *Medical Aspects of Human Sexuality,* Vol. 7, No. 4, 1973.

Fleming, A. T. *For the First Time.* Berkeley: Medallion Books, 1976.

Ford, C. S., and F. A. Beach. *Patterns of Sexual Behavior.* New York: Harper & Row, 1951.

Fortune, R. F. *Sorcerers of Dobu.* New York: E. P. Dutton & Co., 1932.

Fox, J. R. "Sibling Incest," *British Journal of Sociology,* 13:128, 1962.

Franzblau, A. N. "Religion and Sexuality," *Comprehensive Textbook of Psychiatry,* second edition, edited by A. Freedman and H. Kaplan. Baltimore: Williams & Wilkins, 1975.

Freud, A. "Adolescence as a Developmental Disturbance," *Adolescence: Psychosocial Perspectives,* edited by G. Kaplan and S. Lebovici. New York: Basic Books, 1969.

Freud, S. "Civilization and Its Discontents," *Standard Edition of* the *Complete Psychological Works of Sigmund Freud,* Vol. 19. London: Hogarth Press, 1961.

————. "The Future of an Illusion." *Standard Edition of the Complete Psychological Works of Sigmund Freud.* Vol. 21. London: Hogarth Press, 1961.

————. *Introductory Lectures on Psychoanalysis,* "Lecture XX: The Sexual Life of Human Beings," *Standard Edition of the Complete Psychological Works of Sigmund Freud,* Vol. 16. London: Hogarth Press, 1918.

————. "On Narcissism," *Standard Edition of the Complete Psychological Works of Sigmund Freud,* Vol. 14. London: Hogarth Press, 1957.

————. "Some Psychical Consequences of the Anatomical Distinction Between the Sexes," *Standard Edition of the Complete Psychological Works of Sigmund Freud,* Vol. 19. London: Hogarth Press, 1961.

————. "Three Essays on the Theory of Sexuality," *Standard Edition of the Complete Psychological Works of Sigmund Freud,* Vol. 7. London: Hogarth Press, 1953.

Furnas, J. C. *Anatomy of Paradise.* New York: William Sloane Associates, 1948.

Gallup, G. H. *The Gallup Poll of Public Opinion 1935–1971,* Vol. 3. New York: Random House, 1973.

Ginott, H. *Between Parent and Child.* New York: Avon Books, 1969.

Glick, P. C. *American Families.* New York: Wiley, 1967.

Goldfarb, W. "Emotional and Intellectual Consequences of Psychologic Deprivation in Infancy: A Reevaluation," *Psychopathology,* edited by Hoch and Zubin. New York: Grune and Stratton, 1955.

Goodall, J. *The Behavior of Free Living Chimpanzees in the Gombe Stream Reserve,* Animal Monographs, 1958.

Goren, C. C., M. Sarty, and P. Wu. "Visual Following and Pattern Discrimination of Facelike Stimuli by Newborn Infants," *Pediatrics,* Vol. 56, No. 4, 1975.

Gould, R. "Socio-Cultural Roles of Male and Female," *Comprehensive Textbook of Psychiatry*, second edition, edited by A. Freedman and H. Kaplan. Baltimore: Williams & Wilkins, 1975.

Green, W. A. "Early Object Relations, Somatic, Affective and Personal," *Journal of Nervous Mental Disorders*, 126:225–253, 1958.

Greenacre, P. "The Predisposition to Anxiety," *Psychiatry Quarterly*, Vol. 10:66, 1941.

Greenberg, N. "Atypical Behavior During Infancy: Infant Development in Relation to the Behavior and Personality of the Mother," *The Child and His Family*, edited by J. Anthony and C. Koupernik. New York: Wiley, 1970.

Group for the Advancement of Psychiatry. *The Psychic Function of Religion in Mental Illness and Health*. New York: G.A.P. Report, 1968.

Haft, J., and H. B. Benjamin. "Foreign Bodies in the Rectum: Some Psychosexual Aspects," *Medical Aspects of Human Sexuality*, Vol. 7, No. 8, 1973.

Harlow, H., and M. Harlow. "Social Deprivation in Monkeys," *Scientific American*, Vol. 207, 1962.

Hayman, C., and C. Lanza. "Sexual Assault on Women and Girls," *American Journal of Obstetrics and Gynecology*, 109: 480, February, 1971.

Heeb, D. O. "Emotion in Man and Animal: An Analysis of the Intuitive Processes of Recognition," *Psychology Review*, 1946, pp. 53–88.

Heiman, J., L. LoPiccolo, and J. LoPiccolo. *Becoming Orgasmic: A Sexual Growth Program for Women*. New Jersey: Prentice-Hall, 1976.

Henderson, D. J. "Incest," *Comprehensive Textbook of Psychiatry*, second edition, edited by A. Freedman and H. Kaplan. Baltimore: Williams & Wilkins, 1975.

Hodgeman, C. "Talks Between Fathers and Sons," *Medical Aspects of Human Sexuality*, Vol. 9, No. 4, 1975.

Hyman, C. Personal communication with author, August, 1976.

Jensen, Gordon. *Youth and Sex: Pleasure and Responsibility.* Chicago: Nelson Hall, 1973.

Jones, E. *The Life and Work of Sigmund Freud.* New York: Basic Books, 1953.

Kahl, J. A. *The American Class Structure.* New York: Rinehart, 1957.

Kanter, R. "Getting It All Together: Some Group Issues in Communes," *American Journal of Orthopsychiatry,* Vol. 42, 1972.

Kaplan, H. *The New Sex Therapy.* New York: Brunner Mazel, 1974.

Kardiner, A. *The Individual and His Society: The Psychodynamics of Primitive Social Organizations.* New York: Columbia University Press, 1939.

Kaufman, I., A. Peck, and C. K. Taguiri. "The Family Constellation and Overt Incestuous Relations Between Father and Daughter," *American Journal of Orthopsychiatry,* 24:266, 1954.

Keller, S. "The Social World of the Urban Slum Child: Some Early Findings," *American Journal of Orthopsychiatry,* Vol. 33, 1963.

Kempe, C. H., and R. E. Helfer. *Helping the Battered Child and His Family.* New York: J. B. Lippincott Co., 1972.

Kerckhoff, A. C. "Social Class Differences in Sexual Attitudes and Behavior," *Medical Aspects of Human Sexuality,* Vol. 8, No. 11, 1974.

Kestenberg, J. "Psychosexual Impact of Childhood Enemas," *Medical Aspects of Human Sexuality,* Vol. 10, No. 1, 1976.

King, S. "Coping and Growth in Adolescence," *Annual Progress in Child Psychiatry, 1973,* edited by S. Chess and A. Thomas. New York: Brunner Mazel, 1974.

Kinsey, A. C. "A Scientist's Responsibility in Sex Education," paper presented at National Association of Biology Teachers in Philadelphia, Re-presented in *Medical Aspects of Human Sexuality,* Vol. 6, No. 5, 1972.

————. "What I Believe," *San Quentin News,* December, 1954. Published in *Medical Aspects of Human Sexuality,* Vol. 6, No. 5, 1972.

Kinsey, A. C., W. B. Pomeroy, and C. E. Martin. *Sexual Behavior in the Human Male.* Philadelphia: W. B. Saunders, 1948.

Kinsey, A. C., W. B. Pomeroy, C. E. Martin, and P. H. Gebhard. *Sexual Behavior in the Human Female.* Philadelphia: W. B. Saunders, 1953.

Kirkendall, L. A. *Premarital Intercourse and Interpersonal Relationships.* New York: Gramercy Publishing Co., 1961.

Kirvan, John (editor). *Human Sexuality: New Directions in American Catholic Thought.* New York: Paulist Press, 1977.

Klaus, M. H., et al. "Maternal Attachment: Importance of the First Post-Partum Days," *New England Journal of Medicine,* Vol. 286, No. 9, 1972.

Klopfer, P. H. "Mother Love: What Turns It On?" *American Science,* 59:404, 1971.

Knobloch, H., and B. Pasamanick. "Some Etiologic and Prognostic Factors in Early Infantile Autism," *Pediatrics* 55(2):182, February, 1975.

Kreitler, H. S. "Children's Concepts of Sexuality and Birth," *Child Development,* 37:363, 1966.

Kris, E. "Some Comments and Observations of Early Autoerotic Activities," *Psychoanalytic Study of the Child,* Vol. 6, 1951.

Kurland, M., W. Layman, and G. Rozan. "Impotence in the Male," *G. P.* 32:112, November, 1965.

Landers, A. Syndicated column, December 26, 1976.

Lang, R. *Birth Books.* Ben Loman, California: Genesis Press, 1972.

Leboyer, F. *Birth Without Violence.* New York: Knopf, 1975.

Lieberman, J. *Sex and Birth Control.* New York: Schocken Books, 1975.

Lipton, M. "Pornography," *Comprehensive Textbook of Psychiatry,* edited by A. Freedman and H. Kaplan. Baltimore: Williams & Wilkins, 1975.

Lowrie, S. H. "Early Marriage: Premarital Pregnancy and Associated Factors," *Journal of Marriage and Family*, 27:48, 1965.

Lustig, N., J. W. Dresser, S. W. Spellman, and T. B. Murray, "Incest, a Family Group Survival Pattern," *Archives of General Psychiatry*, 14:31, 1966.

Lutier, J. "Rôle de facteurs culturels et psycho-sociaux dans les délits incestueux milieu rural," *Annals of Medicine*, leg. 41:80, 1961.

Lystad, Mary, *Millicent the Monster*, New York: Harlan Quist, 1968.

MacDonald, J. M. *Rape—Offenders and Their Victims*. New York: Charles C. Thomas, 1971.

Maclean, P. "Brain Mechanisms of Elemental Sexual Functions," *Comprehensive Textbook of Psychiatry*, second edition, edited by A. Freedman and H. Kaplan. Baltimore: Williams & Wilkins, 1975.

Mace, D. R. "In Defense of Bundling," *Medical Aspects of Human Sexuality*. Vol. 6, No. 4, 1972.

Malfetti, J., and A. Rubin. "Sex Education: Who is Teaching the Teacher?" *College Record*, 69:214, 1967.

Malinowski, B. *The Sexual Life of Savages in Northwestern Melanesia*. New York: Halcyon House, 1941.

Malmquist, C. P. "Premonitory Signs of Homicidal Aggression in Juveniles," *American Journal of Psychiatry*, Vol. 128, No. 4, 1971.

Marcotte, N., N. Carlson, and D. F. Weiss, "Women's Misunderstandings About Male Sexuality," *Medical Aspects of Human Sexuality*, Vol. 10, No. 12, 1976.

Marmor, J., ed. *Sexual Inversion*. New York: Basic Books, 1965.

Marmor, J., D. W. Bernard, and D. Ottingberg. "Psycho-dynamics of Those in Opposition to Health Programs," *American Journal of Orthopsychiatry*, 30:330, 1960.

Marshall, D. S., and R. C. Suggs. *Human Sexual Behavior*. New York: Basic Books Inc., 1971.

Masters, R. E. L. *Patterns of Incest*, New York: Julian, 1963.

Masters, W. "New Developments in Sex Therapy," presented at American Psychiatric Association Meeting, 1975.

Masters, W., and V. Johnson. *Human Sexual Inadequacy*. Boston: Little, Brown and Company, 1970.

————. *Human Sexual Response.* Boston: Little, Brown and Company, 1966.

Masterson, J. F. *The Psychiatric Dilemma of Adolescence*. Boston: Little, Brown and Company, 1967.

Maxwell, R. J. "Evolution of Sexuality," *Medical Aspects of Human Sexuality*, Vol. 7, No. 10, 1973.

Mead, M. *From the South Seas* (includes *Coming of Age in Samoa, Growing Up in New Guinea,* and *Sex and Temperament*). New York: William Morrow and Company, 1939.

————. *Male and Female*. New York: Dell Publishing Co., 1949.

Mead, M., and M. Wolfenstein. *Childhood in Contemporary Cultures*. Chicago: University of Chicago Press, 1955.

Messenger, J. "Sex and Repression in an Irish Folk Community," *Human Sexual Behavior*, edited by Marshall and Suggs. New York: Basic Books, 1971.

Miller, D. "Violence," *Audio Digest Foundation*, Vol. 2, No. 19.

Money, J. "Sex Hormones and Other Variables in Human Eroticism," *Sex and Internal Secretions*, edited by W. C. Young and G. W. Corner, third edition, Vol. II. Baltimore: Williams & Wilkins, 1961.

Money, J., and A. A. Erhardt. "Exposure: Possible Effects on Behavior in Man," edited by E. P. Michael. *Endocrinology and Human Behavior*. London: Oxford University Press, 1968.

Murdock, G. *The Social Regulation of Sexual Behavior in Psychosexual Development in Health and Disease*, edited by Hoch and Zubin. New York: Grune and Stratton, 1949.

Murdock, G. *Social Structure*. New York: Macmillan, 1960.

Nelson, W. E. *Textbook of Pedriatrics*, eighth edition. Philadelphia: W. B. Saunders & Co., 1964.

Newson, J., and E. Newson. *Four Years Old in an Urban Community*. London: Allen and Unwin, 1968.

Newton, W., and M. Newton. "Medical Progress: Psychologic Aspects of Lactation," *New England Journal of Medicine*, 277:1179–1188, 1967.

Noy, P., S. Wollstein, and A. Kaplan-de-Nour. "Clinical Observations on the Pathogenesis of Impotence," *British Journal of Medical Psychology*, 39:43, 1966.

Opler, M. *An Apache Life Way*. Chicago: University of Chicago Press, 1941.

————. "Anthropological and Cross-Cultural Aspects of Homosexuality," *Sexual Inversion*, edited by J. Marmor. New York: Basic Books, 1965.

————. "Sexual Dysfunctions in Primitive vs. Modern Cultures," *Medical Aspects of Human Sexuality*, Vol. 9, No. 6, 1975.

————. "The Southern Ute Indians in Colorado," *Acculturation in Seven American Indian Tribes*, edited by R. Linton. New York: Appleton-Century-Crofts, 1940.

Owen, F. "Incest—Taboo or Overfamiliarity?" *Medical Aspects of Human Sexuality*, Vol. 8, No. 1, 1974.

Paine, R. S. "The Contribution of Developmental Neurology to Child Psychiatry," *Journal of the American Academy of Child Psychiatry*, 4:353, 1965.

Partridge, C. R. "Immature Character Development," *Journal of Clinical Psychology*, Vol. 5, No. 1, 1976.

Pasamanick, B., and H. Knobloch, "Epidemiological Studies on the Complication of Pregnancy and the Birth Process," *Psychopathology of Childhood*, edited by S. F. Harrison and J. F. McDermott. New York: International Universities Press, 1972.

Piaget, J. *The Origins of Intelligence in Children*. New York: International Universities Press, 1952.

Pomeranz, V., and D. Schultz. *The Mother's Medical Encyclopedia*. New York: Signet Books, 1972.

Poznanski, E., and P. Blos. "Incest," *Medical Aspects of Human Sexuality*, Vol. 9, No. 10, 1975.

Rabban, M. "Sex Role Identification in Young Children in Two Diverse Social Groups," *Genetic Psychology Monographs*, 1950, Vol. 42, pp. 81–158.

Racy, J. "How the 'Work Ethic' Influences Sexuality," *Medical Aspects of Human Sexuality*, Vol. 8, No. 4, 1974.

Rada, R. "Alcohol and Rape," *Medical Aspects of Human Sexuality*, Vol. 9, No. 3, 1975.

Radcliffe-Brown, A. R. *The Andaman Islanders*. New York: Free Press, 1948.

Rainwater, L. *And the Poor Get Children*. Chicago: Quadrangle, 1960.

Ramsey, C. V. "The Sexual Development of Boys," *American Journal of Psychology*, 56:217–233, 1943.

Rank, B., M. C. Putnam, and G. Rocklin. "The Significance of 'Emotional Climate' in Early Feeding Difficulties," *Psychosomatic Medicine*, Vol. 10, 1948.

Rank, O. *"The Trauma of Birth,"* New York: Robert Brunner, 1952.

Raphling, D., B. Carpenter, and A. Davis. "Incest, a Genealogical Study," *Archives of General Psychiatry*, 16:505, 1967.

Rasmussen, A. "The Importance of Sexual Attacks on Children Less Than Fourteen Years of Age for the Development of Mental Diseases and Character Anomalies," *Actu-Psychiatrica-Neurologica*, 9:351, 1934.

Reese, H. W. "Attitudes Toward the Opposite Sex in Late Childhood," *Merrill Palmer Quarterly*, Vol. 12, 1966.

Reiss, I. L. *The Social Context of Premarital Sexual Permissiveness*. New York: Holt, Rinehart & Winston, 1967.

Reuben, D. *Everything You Always Wanted to Know About Sex*. New York: David McKay Co., 1969.

Riemer, S. A. "A Research Note on Incest," *American Journal of Sociology*, 45:554, 1940.

Ringler, N. M., et al. "Mother to Child Speech at Two Years— Effects of Early Post Natal Contact," *Journal of Pediatrics*, Vol. 86, No. 1, 1975.

Robson, K. S. "The Role of Eye-to-Eye Contact in Maternal-Infant Attachment," *Journal of Child Psychology and Psychiatry*, Vol. 8, No. 12, 1967.

Rogawski, A. "How Children Affect the Marital Sexual Relationship," *Medical Aspects of Human Sexuality*, Vol. 10, No. 6, 1976.

Roheim, G. *Children of the Desert.* New York: Basic Books, 1974.

Rutter, M. "Normal Psychosexual Development," *Journal of Child Psychiatry*, Vol. 11, 1971.

Salk, L. *What Every Child Would Like His Parents to Know.* New York: Warner, 1973.

Sarles, R. "Incest," *Pediatric Clinics of North America*, Vol. 22, No. 3, August, 1975.

Schaffer, R. R., and R. Callender. "Psychological Effects of Hospitalization in Infancy," *Pediatrics*, Vol. 24, 1959.

Schlacter, M., and S. A. Cotte, "A Medical Physiological and Social Study of Incest From a Pedopsychiatric Point of View," *Acta Paedopsychiat*, 27:139, 1960.

Schwab, J. "The Difficulties of Being Wife, Mistress, and Mother," *Medical Aspects of Human Sexuality*, Vol. 8, No. 5, 1974.

Schwarz, G. "Devices to Prevent Masturbation," *Journal of Human Sexuality*, Vol. 7, No. 5, 1973.

Sears, R., E. Macoby, and A. Levin. *Patterns of Child Rearing.* New York: Harper & Row, 1957.

Seiden, A. "Overview, Research on the Psychology of Women," *American Journal of Psychiatry*, Vol. 133, No. 10, 1976.

Skopec, H. M., S. D. Rosenberg, and G. J. Tucker. "Sexual Behavior in Schizophrenia," *Medical Aspects of Human Sexuality*, Vol. 10, No. 4, 1976.

Sloane, P. S., and Karpinski, E. "Effects of Incest Upon the Participants," *American Journal of Psychiatry*, 12:666, 1952.

Small, I. P., and J. G. Small. "Sexual Behavior and Mental Illness," *Comprehensive Textbook of Psychiatry*, Vol. II, edited by A. Freedman and H. Kaplan. Baltimore: Williams & Wilkins, 1974.

Smith, J. W. "Libido of Female Alcoholics," *Medical Aspects of Human Sexuality*, Vol. 9, No. 9, 1975.

Smith, M. Personal communication with author, August, 1976.

Sontag, L. W., "Differences in Modifiability of Fetal Behavior and Physiology," *Psychosomatic Medicine*, 6:151–154, 1944.

————. "The Significance of Fetal Environmental Differences," *American Journal of Obstetrics, Gynecology*, 42:996–1003, 1941.

Sorenson, R. C. *Adolescent Sexuality in Contemporary America: Personal Values and Sexual Behavior*. New York: World Publishing, 1973.

Spitz, R. A. "The Role of Early Sexual Behavior Patterns in Personality Formation," *Psychoanalytic Study of the Child*, Vol. 17, 1962.

————. "Hospitalism, an Inquiry into the Genesis of Psychiatric Conditions in Early Childhood," *Psychoanalytic Study of the Child*, 1:53, 1945.

Spock, B. *Baby and Child Care*. New York: Pocket Books, 1968 and 1976.

Stephens, W. *The Family in Cross-Cultural Perspective*. New York: Holt, Rinehart & Winston, 1963.

Stern, D. N. "A Microanalysis of Mother-Infant Interaction," *Journal of the American Academy of Child Psychiatry*, 10:501, 1971.

Stiles, H. R. *Bundling: Its Origin, Progress and Decline in America*. New York: Book Collectors Association, 1934. (Reprint)

Task Force Report 8. *Clinical Aspects of the Violent Individual*. Washington, D. C.: American Psychiatric Association, 1974.

Thomas, A., H. G. Birch, S. Chess, M. E. Hertzig, and S. Korn. *Behavioral Individuality in Early Childhood*. New York: New York University Press, 1965.

Tormeys, Y. M. *Child Victims of Incest.* Denver, Colorado: American Humane Association.

Udry, J. "Sex and Family Life," *Medical Aspects of Human Sexuality,* Vol. 2, No. 11, Nov. 1968.

Waggoner, R. "Half of all marriages have sexual problems," commentary in *Medical Aspects of Human Sexuality,* Vol. 8, No. 11, 1974.

Wahl, C. W. "The Psychodynamics of Consummated Maternal Incest," *Archives of General Psychiatry,* 3:188, 1960.

Wallin, R., and R. P. Riley. "Reactions of Mothers to Pregnancy and Adjustment to Offspring in Infancy," *American Journal Orthopsychiatry,* 20:616, 1950.

Walters, J., and R. Cannon. "Interaction of Mothers and Children From Lower-Class Families," *Child Development,* Vol. 35, 1964.

Warner, W. L. *A Black Civilization.* New York: Harper & Row, 1937.

Weinberg, S. K. *Incest Behavior.* New York: Citadel Press, 1955.

Weiner, I. B. "Father-daughter Incest, a Clinical Report," *Psychiatric Quarterly,* 36:607, 1962.

Weiner, I. B. "Incest: A Survey," *Excerpta Criminologica,* 4:137, 1964.

Weisman, A. D. "Self-Destruction and Sexual Perversion," in E. S. Schneidman, *Essays in Self Destruction.* New York: Science House, 1967.

White, M. S. "Social Class, Child Rearing Practices and Child Behavior," *American Sociological Review,* Vol. 22, 1957.

White, R. W. "Motivation Reconsidered: The Concept of Competence," *Psychology Review,* 66:5, 1959.

Whiting, J. W., and I. L. Child. *Child Training and Personality: A Cross-Cultural Study.* New Haven: Yale University Press, 1953.

Winnecott, D. W. *Playing and Reality.* London: Tavistock, 1971.

Wolfenstein, M. *The Emergence of Fun Morality in Mass Leisure,* edited by E. Lanabee and R. Meyerson. Chicago: The Free Press, 1958.

Wolfenstein, M. "Trends in Infant Care," *American Journal of Orthopsychiatry,* Vol. 23, 1953.

Yorukoglu, A., and J. Kemph. "Children Not Severely Damaged by Incest With a Parent," *American Academy of Child Psychiatry,* 5:111, 1966.

INDEX